M000197256

The Journals of
Robert Rogers
of the Rangers

The Journals of
Robert Rogers
of the Rangers

The Exploits of Rogers & the Rangers
from 1755-1761 in the French &
Indian War in His Own Words

LEONAUR

The Journals of Robert Rogers of the Rangers: The Exploits of Rogers & the Rangers from 1755-1761 in the French & Indian Wars in His Own Words

Published by Leonaur Ltd

Material original to this edition and its origination in
this form copyright © 2005 Leonaur Ltd

ISBN (10 digit): 1-84677-010-6 (hardcover)
ISBN (13 digit): 978-1-84677-010-4 (hardcover)

ISBN (10 digit): 1-84677-002-5 (softcover)
ISBN (13 digit): 978-1-84677-002-9 (softcover)

http://www.leonaur.com

Publishers Notes

In the interests of authenticity, the spellings, grammar and place names used
in this book have been retained from the original edition.

The opinions of the author represent a view of events in which he was a
participant related from his own perspective;
as such the text is relevant as an historical document.

The views expressed in this book are not necessarilty
those of the publisher.

An Introduction by Robert Rogers
Upon the Publication of His Journals

It would be offering an affront to the public, should I pretend to have no private views in publishing the following Journals: but they will excuse me if I leave them to conjecture what my particular views are, and claim the merit of impartially relating matters of fact, without disguise or equivocation. Most of those which relate to myself can at present be attested by living witnesses.

And should the troubles in America be renewed, and the savages repeat those scenes of barbarity they so often have acted on the British subjects, which there is so great reason to believe will happen, I flatter myself, that such as are immediately concerned may reap some advantages from these pages.

Should any one take offence at what they may here meet with, before they venture upon exhibiting a charge, they are desired, in favour of themselves, to consider, that I am in a situation where they cannot attack me to their own advantage; that it is the soldier, not the scholar that writes; and that things here were wrote, not with silence and leisure, but in desarts, on rocks and mountains, amidst the hurries, disorders, and noise of war, and under that depression of spirits, which is the natural consequence of exhausting fatigue. This was my situation when the following journals or accounts were transmitted to the generals and commanders I acted under, which I am not now at liberty to correct except in some very gross and palpable errors.

It would perhaps gratify the curious to have a particular account of my life, preceding the war; but tho' I could easily indulge them herein, without any dishonour to myself, yet I beg they will be content with my relating only such circumstances and occurrences as led me to a knowledge of many parts of the country, and tended in some measure to qualify me for the service I have since been employed in. Such, in particular, was the situation of the place in which I received my early education, a frontier town in the province of New Hampshire, where I could hardly avoid obtaining some knowledge of the manners, customs, and language of the Indians, as many of them resided in the neighbourhood, and daily conversed and dealt with the English.

Between the years 1743 and 1755 my manner of life was such as led me to a general acquaintance both with the British and French settlements in North America, and especially with the uncultivated desart, the mountains, valleys, rivers, lakes, and several passes that lay between and contiguous to the said settlements. Nor did I content myself with the accounts I received from the Indians, or the information of hunters, but travelled over large tracts of the country myself, which tended not more to gratify my curiosity, than to inure me to hardships, and, without vanity I may say, to qualify me for the very service I have since been employed in.

About this time the proceedings of the French in America were such as excited the jealousy of the English, especially in New York and New England; and as Crown Point was the place from which, for many years, the Indians in the French interest had been fitted out against our settlements on the frontiers, a design was formed in the beginning of 1755 to dispossess them of that post; pursuant to which troops were levied in the several provinces of New England, New York and New Jersey.

The general rendezvous was appointed as Albany in the province of New York, and the troops put under the command of Major General (since Sir William) Johnson.

I had the honour of commanding a company in the troops

furnished by the province of New Hampshire, with which I made several excursions, pursuant to special orders from the governor of that province, on the northern and western frontiers, with a view to deter the French and their Indians from making inroads upon us that way.

In this manner I was employed till the month of July, when I received orders to repair to Albany, at which place I tarried till August 26th, and was then ordered with 100 men to escort the provision-waggons from thence to the Carrying-Place, then so called, since Fort Edward. Here I waited upon the General, to whom I was recommended as a person well acquainted with the haunts and passes of the enemy, and the Indian method of fighting, and was by him dispatched with small parties on several tours towards the French posts, and was on one of these up Hudson's River on the 8th of September, when Baron Dieskau was made prisoner, and the French and Indians under his command defeated, at the south-end of Lake George.

The 24th of September I received orders from the General to proceed with four men to Crown Point, and, if practicable, to bring a prisoner from thence; and with an account of the manner in which I executed these orders I shall begin my Journals.

A Journal, &c
September 24, 1755

Pursuant to the orders of this date from Major-General Johnson, Commander in Chief of the Provincial Forces, raised for the reduction of Crown Point, I embarked with four men upon Lake George, to reconnoitre the strength of the enemy, and proceeding down the lake twenty-five miles, I landed on the west-side, leaving two men in charge of the boat, while I marched with the other two till the 29th, when I had a fair view of the fort at Crown Point, and discovered a large body of Indians round the fort, and, supposed they were shooting at marks, (a diversion much in use among the savages).

At night I crept through the enemy's guards into a small village lying south of the fort, and passed their centries to an eminence south-west of it, from whence I discovered they were building a battery, and had already thrown up an entrenchment on that side of the fort.

The next day, from an eminence at a small distance from the former, I discovered an encampment, which extended from the fort south-east to a wind-mill, at about thirty yards distance; as near as I could judge, their number amounted to about 500 men: but finding no opportunity to procure a captive, and that our small party was discovered, I judged it proper to begin a retreat homeward the 1st of October.

I took my route within two miles of Ticonderoga, from whence I observed a large smoak to arise, and heard the explosion of a number of small arms; but our provisions being expended, we could not tarry to ascertain the number of the enemy there.

On the 2d we arrived at the place where we left our boat

11

in the charge of two men, but to our great mortification found they were gone, and no provisions left. This circumstance hastened us to the encampment with all possible speed, where we arrived the 4th, not a little fatigued and distressed with hunger and cold.

October 7, 1755

I received orders of this date from General Johnson, to embark with five men under my command to reconnoitre the French troops at Ticonderoga.

Accordingly I proceeded at night to a point of land on the west side of the lake, where we landed, hid our canoe, and left two men in charge of it.

The next day, with the other three, I marched to the point at Ticonderoga, where we arrived about noon. I here observed a body of men, which I judged to be about 2000 in number, who had thrown up an entrenchment, and prepared large quantities of hewn timber in the adjacent woods.

We remained here the second night, and next morning saw them lay the foundation of a fort, on the point which commands the pass from Lake George to Lake Champlain, and the entrance of South Bay, or Wood Creek.

Having made what discoveries we could, we began our return, in which we found that the enemy had a large advanced guard at the north end of Lake George, where the river issues out of it into Lake Champlain. While we were viewing there, I observed a bark-canoe with nine Indians and a Frenchman in it, going up the lake. We kept sight of them till they passed the point of land where our canoe and men were left, where, when we arrived, we had information from our people that the above Indians and Frenchman had landed on an island six miles to the south of us, near the middle of the lake.

In a short time after, we saw them put off from the island, and steer directly towards us; upon which we put ourselves in readiness to receive them in the best manner we could, and gave them a salute at about 100 yards distance, which reduced their number to four. We then took boat and pursued them down the lake, till they were relieved by two canoes, which obliged us to retreat towards our encampment at Lake George, where we arrived the 10th October.

October 15, 1755

Agreeable to orders of this date from General Johnson, I embarked with forty men in five boats. Our design was to discover the strength of the enemy's advanced guard, and, if possible, to decoy the whole, or part of them, into an ambush; but tho' we were indefatigable in our endeavours for several days, yet all our attempts of this kind proved abortive; and, as an account of our several movements during this scout would little gratify the reader, I shall omit giving a particular detail of them. We returned safe to our encampment at Lake George on the 19th.

October 21, 1755

I had orders from General Johnson of this date, to embark for Crown Point, with a party of four men, in quest of a prisoner.

At night we landed on the west-side of Lake George, twenty-five miles from the English camp. The remainder of the way we marched by land, and the 26th came in sight of the fort.

In the evening we approached nearer, and next morning found ourselves within about 300 yards of it. My men lay concealed in a thicket of willows, while I crept something nearer, to a large pine-log, where I concealed myself by holding bushes in my hand.

Soon after sun-rise the soldiers issued out in such numbers, that my men and I could not possibly join each other without a discovery. About 10 o'clock a single man marched out directly towards our ambush. When I perceived him within ten yards of me, I sprung over the log, and met him, and offered him quarters, which he refused, and made a pass at me with a dirk, which I avoided, and presented my fusee to his breast; but notwithstanding, he still pushed on with resolution, and obliged me to dispatch him. This gave an alarm to the enemy, and made it necessary for us to hasten to the mountain. I arrived safe at our camp the 30th, with all my party.

November 4, 1755

Agreeable to orders from General Johnson this day, I embarked for the enemy's advanced guard before mentioned, with a party of thirty men, in four battoes, mounted with two wall-pieces each.

The next morning, a little before day-light, we arrived within half a mile of them, where we landed, and concealed our boats; I then sent out four men as spies, who returned the next evening, and informed me, that the enemy had no works round them, but lay entirely open to an assault; which advice I dispatched immediately to the General, desiring a sufficient force to attack them, which, notwithstanding the General's earnestness and activity in the affair, did not arrive till we were obliged to retreat.

On our return, however, we were met by a reinforcement, sent by the General, whereupon I returned again towards the enemy, and the next evening sent two men to see if the enemy's centries were alert, who approached so near as to be discovered and fired at by them, and were so closely pursued in their retreat, that unhappily our whole party was discovered.

The first notice I had of this being the case, was from two canoes with thirty men in them, which I concluded came out with another party by land, in order to force us between two fires; to prevent which, I with Lieutenant McCurdy, and fourteen men, embarked in two boats, leaving the remainder of the party on the shore, under the command of Captain Putnam.

In order to decoy the enemy within the reach of our wall-pieces, we steered as if we intended to pass by them, which luckily answered our expectations; for they boldly headed us till within about an hundred yards, when we discharged the before mentioned pieces, which killed several of them, and put the rest to flight, in which we drove them so near where our land-party lay, that they were again galled by them; several of the enemy were tumbled into the water, and their canoes rendered very leaky. At this time I discovered their party by land, and gave our people notice of it, who thereupon embarked likewise, without receiving any considerable injury from the enemy's fire, notwithstanding it was for some time very brisk upon them. We warmly pursued the enemy, and again got an opportunity to discharge our wall-pieces upon them, which confused them much, and obliged them to disperse. - We pursued them down the lake to their landing, where they were received and covered by 100 men, upon whom we discharged our wall pieces, and obliged them to retire; but finding their number vastly superior to our's, we judged it most prudent to return to our encampment at Lake George, where we safely arrived on the 8th of November.

November 10, 1755

Pursuant to orders I received this day from Gen. Johnson, in order to discover the enemy's strength and situation at Ticonderoga, I proceeded on the scout with a party of ten men, on the 12th instant, and on the 14th arrived within view of the fort at that place, and found they had erected three new barracks and four store-houses in the fort, between which and the water they had eighty battoes hauled upon the beach, and about fifty tents near the fort; they appeared to be very busy at work.

Having by these discoveries answered the design of our march, we returned, and arrived at our encampment the 19th of November.

December 19, 1755

Having had a month's repose, I proceeded, agreeable to orders from General Johnson, with two men, once more to reconnoitre the French at Ticonderoga.

In our way we discovered a fire upon an island, adjacent to the route we took, which, as we supposed had been kindled by some of the enemy who were there. This obliged us to lie by and act like fishermen, the better to deceive them, till night came on, when we proceeded and retired to the west-side of the lake, fifteen miles north of the fort. Here concealing our boat, the 20th we pursued our march by land, and on the 21st, at noon, were in sight of the French fort, where we found their people still deeply engaged at work, and discovered four pieces of cannon mounted on the south-east bastion, two at the north-west towards the woods, and two on the south.

By what I judged, the number of their troops were about 500.

I made several attempts to take a prisoner, by way-laying their paths; but they always passed in numbers vastly superior to mine, and thereby disappointed me.

We approached very near their fort by night, and were driven by the cold (which was now very severe) to take shelter in one of their evacuated huts; before day, there was a fall of snow, which obliged us with all possible speed to march homeward, lest the enemy should perceive our tracks and pursue us.

We found our boat in safety, and had the good fortune (after being almost exhausted with hunger, cold, and fatigue) to kill two deer, with which being refreshed, on the 24th we returned to Fort William Henry (a fortress erected in this year's campaign) at the south end of Lake George.

About this time General Johnson retired to Albany, to which place commissioners were sent from the several governments whose troops had been under his command (New Hampshire only excepted). These commissioners were empowered by their respective constituents, with the assent of a council of war, to garrison Fort William Henry and Fort Edward, for that winter, with part of the troops that had served the preceding year.

Accordingly a regiment was formed, to which Boston government furnished a Colonel - Connecticut a Lieutenant-Colonel - and New York a Major: after which it was adjudged, both by Gen. Johnson and these Commissioners, that it would be of great use to leave one company of woodsmen or Rangers under my command, to make excursions towards the enemy's forts during the winter; I accordingly remained, and did duty the whole winter, until called upon by General Shirley.

January 14, 1756

I this day marched with a party of seventeen men, to reconnoitre the French forts; we proceeded down the lake, on the ice, upon skaits, and halted for refreshment near the fall out of Lake George into Lake Champlain.

At night we renewed our march, and, by day-break on the 16th, formed an ambush on a point of land on the east-shore of Lake Champlain, within gun-shot of the path in which the enemy passed from one fort to the other.

About sun-rise, two sledges laden with fresh beef were presented to our view, we intercepted the drivers, destroyed their loading, and afterwards returned to Fort William Henry, where I arrived with my prisoners and party in good health the 17th.

January 26, 1756

Pursuant to orders of this date, from Colonel Glasier, I marched from Lake George with a party of fifty men, with a design to discover the strength and works of the enemy at Crown Point.

On the 2d of February, we arrived within a mile of that fortress, where we climbed a very steep mountain, from which we had a clear and full prospect of the fort, and an opportunity of taking a plan of the enemy's works there. In the evening we retired to a small village, half a mile from the fort, and formed an ambuscade on each side of the road leading from the fort to the village.

Next morning a Frenchman fell into our hands; soon after we discovered two more, but they unluckily got sight of us before they were in our power, and hastily retired to the fort.

Finding ourselves discovered by the enemy by this accident, we employed ourselves while we dare stay in setting fire to the houses and barns of the village, with which were consumed large quantities of wheat, and other grain; we also killed about fifty cattle, and then retired, leaving the whole village in flames, and arrived safe at our fort, with our prisoner, the 6th of February.

February 29, 1756

Agreeable to orders from Colonel Glasier, I this day marched with a party of fifty-six men down the west-side of Lake George. We continued our route northward till the 5th of March, and then steered east to Lake Champlain, about six miles north of Crown Point, where, by the intelligence we had from the Indians, we expected to find some inhabited villages.

We then attempted to cross the lake, but found the ice too weak.

The 17th we returned and marched round the bay to the west of Crown Point, and at night got into the cleared land among their houses and barns; here we formed an ambush, expecting their labourers out to tend their cattle, and clean their grain, of which there were several barns full; we continued there that night, and next day till dark, when, discovering none of the enemy, we set fire to the houses and barns, and marched off.

In our return I took a fresh view of Ticonderoga, and reconnoitred the ground between that fort and the advanced guard on Lake George, approaching so near as to see their centries on the ramparts, and obtained all the knowledge of their works, strength, and situation, that I desired.

The 14th of March, we returned safe to Fort William Henry. The next day, after my return from this scout, I received a letter, dated February 24, 1756, from Mr. William Alexander of New York, who was secretary to Mr. Shirley, Commander in chief of the troops at Oswego the preceding year, and who now, upon the decease of General Braddock, succeeded to the chief command of all his Majesty's forces in North America, and was now at Boston, preparing for the ensuing campaign, being previously recommended to this gentleman by General Johnson.

I was desired by the above-mentioned letter to wait on him at Boston; of which I informed the commanding officer at the fort, and, with his approbation, I set out on the 17th of March, leaving the command of my company to Mr. Noah Johnson, my Ensign; my brother Richard Rogers, who was my Lieutenant, being sent to Boston by the commanding officer, on some dispatches previous to this.

On the 23d, I waited on the General, and met with a very friendly reception; he soon intimated his design of giving me the command of an independent company of Rangers, and the very next morning I received the commission, with a set of instructions.

According to the General's orders, my company was to consist of sixty privates, at 3s. New York currency per day, three serjeants at 4s. an Ensign at 5s. a Lieutenant at 7s. and my own pay was fixed at 10s. per day. Ten Spanish dollars were allowed to each man towards providing cloaths, arms and blankets.

My orders were to raise this company as quick as possible, to inlist none but such as were used to travelling and hunting, and in whose courage and fidelity I could confide; they were, moreover, to be subject to military discipline, and the articles of war.

Our rendezvous was appointed at Albany, from thence to proceed in four whale-boats to Lake George, and, "from time to time, to use my best endeavours to distress the French and their allies, by sacking, burning, and destroying their houses, barns barracks, canoes battoes &c. and by killing their cattle of every kind; and at all times to endeavour to way-lay, attack, and destroy their convoys of provisions by land and water in any part of the country, where I could find them.

With these instructions, I received letters to the commanding officers, at Fort William-Henry and Fort Edward, directing them to forward the service, with which I was now particularly charged.

When my company was completed, a part marched under the command of Lieutenant Rogers to Albany; with the remainder, I was ordered to march through the woods to No.4, then a frontier town greatly exposed to the enemy.

April 28, 1756

I received orders to march from thence to Crown Point, in pursuance of which we travelled through desarts and mountains. The second day of our march, my second Lieutenant, Mr. John Stark, was taken sick, and obliged to return, with whom I sent six men to guard him to Fort Edward.

We continued our march till the 5th of May, when I arrived with nine men at Lake Champlain, four miles south of Crown Point. Here we concealed our packs, and marched up to a village on the east-side, about two miles distant from Crown Point, but found no inhabitant there. We lay in wait the whole day following, opposite to Crown Point, expecting some party to cross the lake; but nothing appeared except about four or five hundred men in canoes and battoes, coming up the lake from St. John's to Crown Point.

We kept our stations till next day, ten o'clock a.m. to observe the motions of the enemy, but finding no opportunity to trap any of them, we killed twenty three head of cattle, the tongues of which was a very great refreshment to us on our journey.

We at this time discovered eleven canoes manned with a considerable number of French and Indians crossing the lake directly towards us, upon which we retired; and the better to escape our pursuers we dispersed, each man taking a different route.

We afterwards assembled at the place where we concealed our packs, and on a raft crossed over to the west-side of the lake. In our way we had a view of the French and Indians, encamped at the old Indian carrying-place, near Ticonderoga, and the 11th of May arrived safe at Fort William-Henry.

Mr. Stark, with his party, arrived at Fort Edward three days before. In their way they discovered a scouting party of three or four hundred Indians. Lieutenant Rogers with his party had arrived some days before this, and was at this time out upon a scout.

May 20, 1756

Agreeable to orders from the General, I set out with a party of eleven men to reconnoitre the French advanced guards.

The next day, from the top of a mountain, we had a view of them, and judged their number to be about 300; they were busy in fortifying themselves with palisadoes.

From the other side of the mountain we had a prospect of Ticonderoga fort, and, from the ground their encampment took up, I judged it to consist of about 1000 men.

This night we lodged on the mountain, and next morning marched to the Indian carrying-path, that leads from Lake George to Lake Champlain, and formed an ambuscade between the French guards and Ticonderoga fort.

About six o'clock 118 Frenchmen passed by without discovering us; in a few minutes after, twenty-two more came the same road, upon whom we fired, killed six, and took one prisoner; but the large party returning obliged us to retire in haste, and we arrived safe, with our prisoner, at Fort William Henry the 23d.

The prisoner we had taken reported, "that a party of 220 French and Indians were preparing to invest the out-parties at Fort Edward," which occasioned my marching the next morning with a party of 78 men, to join a detachment of Col Bayley's regiment, to scour the woods as far as South Bay, if possible to intercept the enemy; but we could not discover them.

June 13, 1756

Agreeable to orders this evening, I embarked with a party of 26 men in battoes upon Lake George, to revisit the French advanced guard; excessive thunder and lightening obliged us to land at about ten miles distance from our fort, where we spent the night.

The next morning, about sun-rise, we heard the explosion of upwards of twenty small arms, on the opposite side of the lake, which we supposed to be a party of French and Indians, cleaning their guns after the rain.

In the evening we embarked again and early in the morning of the 16th drew up our battoes about four miles distant from the advanced guard, and afterwards lay in ambush by the path leading from thence to a mountain, in order to surprize the enemy, who went there daily in parties, to take a view of the lake; but finding they were not at that place, we marched to the spot where the enemy had posted their advanced guard, but they had retired and demolished all their works there; we then continued our march towards Ticonderoga, near which place we ascended an eminence, and had a clear view of their works.

I judged that their garrison and encampment consisted of about 3000 men.

We then set out on our return, and arrived at Fort William-Henry the 18th instant, except one man, who strayed from us, and did not get in till the 23d, then almost famished for want of sustenance.

About this time the General augmented my company to seventy men, and sent me six light whale-boats from Albany, with orders to proceed immediately to Lake Champlain, to cut off, if possible, the provisions and flying parties of the enemy.

June 28, 1756

I embarked with fifty men in five whale-boats, and proceeded to an island in Lake George.

The next day, at about five miles distance from this island, we landed our boats, and carried them about six miles over a mountain, to South Bay, where we arrived the 3d of July.

The following evening we embarked again, and went down the bay to within six miles of the French fort, where we concealed our boats till evening. We then embarked again, and passed by Ticonderoga undiscovered, tho' we were so near the enemy as to hear his centry's watchword. We judged from the number of their fires, that they had a body of about 2000 men, and the lake in this place to be near 400 yards wide.

About five miles further down, we again concealed our boats, and lay by all day. We saw several battoes going and coming upon the lake.

At night we put off again, with a design to pass by Crown Point, but afterwards judged it imprudent by reason of the clearness of the night, so lay concealed again the next day, when near a hundred boats passed us, seven of which came very near the point where we were, and would have landed there; but the officer insisted, in our hearing, upon going about 150 yards further, where they landed, and dined in our view.

About nine o'clock at night we re-imbarked, and passed the fort at Crown Point, and again concealed our boats at about ten miles distance from it. This day, being July 7th, 30 boats, and a schooner of about 30 or 40 tons, passed by us towards Canada.

We set out again in the evening, and landed about fifteen miles further down, from which place I sent a party for further discovery, who brought intelligence of a schooner at anchor, about a mile from us; we immediately lightened our boats, and prepared to board her; but were prevented by two lighters coming up the lake, who, we found, intended to land where we were posted; these we fired upon, then hailed them, and offered them quarters, if they would come ashore; but they hastily pushed towards the opposite shore, where we pursued and intercepted them: we found their number to be twelve, three of which were killed by our fire, and two wounded, one of them in such a manner that he soon died.

We sunk and destroyed their vessels and cargoes, which consisted chiefly of wheat and flour, wine and brandy; some few casks of the latter we carefully concealed.

The prisoners informed us, that they were part of 500 men, the remainder of which were not far behind on their passage, which induced us to hasten our return to our garrison, where, with our prisoners, we safely arrived the 15th of July.

These prisoners, upon examination, reported, "That a great number of regular troops and militia were assembling at Chamblee, and destined for Carillon or Ticonderoga[*]: that great quantities of provisions were transporting there, and a new General[**] with two regiments lately arrived from France: that there was no talk of any design upon our forts on this side; but that a party of 300 French, and 20 Indians, had already set out to intercept our convoys of provisions between Albany and Lake George: that 60 livres was the reward for an English scalp, and that the prisoners were sold in Canada for 50 crowns each: that their prospect of an harvest was very encouraging, but that the small-pox made great havock amongst the inhabitants."

About the time of my setting out upon this scout, Major General Shirley was superseded in his command by Major General Abercrombie, who arrived at the head-quarters in

---

[*]*The former is the French, the latter the Indian name, signifying the meeting or confluence of three waters.*
[**]*The Marquis de Montcalm, who commanded in the reduction of Oswego this year, and of Fort William Henry the year following.*

Albany on the 25th of June, and brought with him two regiments of regular troops from England.

I therefore, upon my return, wrote to his Excellency, desiring leave to lay before him the minutes of my last scout, and to recommend to his consideration an augmentation of the Rangers. The General permitted me, with my brother Richard Rogers, to wait upon him at Albany. In this interview we discoursed on the subject of my letter, in consequence of which he immediately ordered a new company of Rangers to be raised, and gave the command of it to my brother*, appointed Noah Johnson, my former Ensign, his First Lieutenant, Nathaniel Abbot his Second Lieutenant, and Caleb Page his Ensign. John Stark, formerly my Second Lieutenant, was appointed my First, John McCurdy succeeded to his place, and Jonathan Burbank was appointed my Ensign.

*He compleated his company in 28 days, and, by the General's orders, went up Mohawke river, to serve as a scouting party for the troops that way.

August 2, 1756

Agreeable to orders received of General Abercrombie at Albany, the 23d of July, I embarked this day at Fort William-Henry, on board one of the lighters built there this summer, with twenty-five of my company, in order to reconnoitre the enemy at Ticonderoga and Crown Point, and sixty men under Capt. Larnard of the provincials, who had General Winslow's* orders to proceed with his men to the French advanced guard; but he not being acquainted with the way thither, put himself under my command.

We landed this morning about fifteen miles down Lake George, and proceeded with the party till the 4th in the evening, and encamped about a mile from the advanced guard.

The 5th in the morning mustered the whole party, and got to the summit of a hill, west of the advanced guard, where we discovered two advanced posts, which I then imagined was the whole of the guard, one of them on the west-side, half a mile southward of Lake Champlain, the other on the east-side of the lake, opposite the former, at the old Indian carrying-place. We judged there were about 400 men on the east, and 200 on the west.

After deliberating with Capt, Larnard upon the strength and disposition of the enemy, and the report of our advanced party, we concluded it unadviseable to continue there any longer. He returned towards Fort William-Henry, and I went on with my own party till we came within view of Ticonderoga Fort, where, from an eminence, I discovered the situation, but could not ascertain the strength of it to my satisfaction.

*General Winslow commanded the provincial troops this year, by virtue of a commission from the several provinces, who were concerned in 1755, in the same expedition, and was now the greatest part of the provincial troops at Lake George.

34

August 6th, 1756

I went down towards Crown Point, by the west-side of Lake Champlain, and discovered several battoes passing from that place to Ticonderoga with troops on board. We then proceeded to the place where we burnt the village, as mentioned before, and there encamped, and perceived a party sallying out, driving a number of horses to feed.

The 7th we lay in ambush by the road, with a design to intercept such as might come out to drive in the cattle; but no one appearing for that purpose, we approached nearer, to within half a mile of the fort, where we were discovered by two Frenchmen, before they were in our power. This accident obliged us to make a retreat, in which we killed upwards of forty cattle. We arrived at Fort William-Henry, August 10.

A company of Stockbridge Indians was this year employed in his Majesty's service, commanded by Indian officers, properly commissioned by General Shirley, before he was superseded in his command. General Abercrombie was somewhat at a loss how to dispose of this company, and applied to Sir William Johnson, who advised, that a part[*], viz. thirty privates and a Lieutenant, should scout and scour the woods under my direction, which party had arrived while I was out upon my last scout, and Lieutenant Stark had strengthened their party with some of our people, and sent them out with particular directions what route to take, the day before I arrived.

About this time his Excellency the Earl of Loudoun arrived at Albany, and had taken upon him the command of the army, to whom I applied as I had done before to Gen. Abercrombie, transmitting to him an account of the Indian scout above-

[*]The remainder of this Indian company, with their Captain, were sent to Saratoga, to be under the direction of Colonel Burton.

mentioned (who returned the 13th with two French scalps, agreeable to their barbarous custom) and desiring that with them I might attempt to penetrate into Canada, and distress the inhabitants, by burning their harvest (now nearly ripe) and destroying their cattle.

Accordingly, August 16, we embarked in whale-boats in two departments, the one commanded by Lieutenant Stark, the other by myself.

The next morning we joined each other, at which time also fell in with us a party of eight Mohocks, who had marched out from Fort William-Henry the day before. We then marched directly to the place where we left our whale-boats the 7th of July, proceeding about twenty-five miles northward of Crown Point fort, on the west-side of Lake Champlain, where we all (excepting one man who strayed from us and returned) arrived safe the 24th.

We embarked again in our boats, and steered down the lake towards St. John's.

The 25th we proceeded twenty miles further, and about midnight discovered a schooner standing up the lake with a fair wind towards Crown Point; they passed us so swiftly that we could not possibly board her, as we intended.

The 26th we landed, and the Mohocks left us to join another party of theirs then out on a scout.

The 27th we got on a point, with a design to intercept the enemy's battoes that might pass up and down the lake, but not discovering any, and our provisions growing short, we returned up the lake, and landed eight miles north of the fort at Crown Point, on the east-side of the lake.

The 29th in the morning we marched to a village lying east of the fort, and in our way took prisoners, a man, his wife, and daughter, (a girl about fourteen years of age); with these prisoners we returned, and arrived safe at Fort William-Henry, Sept. 22, 1756.

The man-prisoner, above-mentioned, upon examination,

reported, "That he was born at Vaisac, in the province of Guienne in France: that he had been in Canada about fifteen years, and in the colonies service about six, and two years at Crown Point: that there were only 300 men at Crown Point, and those chiefly inhabitants of the adjacent villages; that there were 4000 men at Ticonderoga or Carillon, 1500 of which were regular troops, who had a sufficiency of all kinds of provisions: that he never was at Ticonderoga or at the advance guard, but heard there were only fifteen men at the latter: that the French had 600 Indians at Ticonderoga, and expected 600 more: that 1200 were arrived at Quebec for Carillon, which last 1800 were under the command of Mons. Scipio de la Masure: that they had a great quantity of cannon, mortars, shells &c. at Ticonderoga, but he did not know the number and quantity: that they expected the above reinforcement in two or three days at Ticonderoga, having sent boats to Montreal to fetch them: that they understood by a letter that Oswego had fallen into their hands, but the news was not confirmed: that they had heard we intended to invest Carillon, but did not know what movements were intended on their side should we neglect it: that they had 150 battoes on Lake Champlain, which were kept at Carillon, thirty-five of which constantly plied between Montreal and that fortress: that Mons. Montcalm commanded at Frontiniac with 5000 men, but did not know whether these troops were regulars or provincials: that a great number of vessels had arrived at Canada with provisions and military stores: that they heard we had several ships in the river St. Lawrence: that Mons. Conte de Levi commanded at Carillon, and came last May from France; and that, since the last two shallops or lighters (before-mentioned) were taken, they had augmented the number of men on board the large schooner in Lake Champlain from twelve to thirty."

Upon my return to the fort, I received orders from my Lord Loudon to wait upon Col. Burton, of the 48th regiment, for instructions, he being then posted at Saratoga. By him I was ordered to return to my company at Fort William-Henry, and march them to the South Bay, thence east to the Wood Creek, then to cross it southerly, opposite Saratoga, and return and make my report to him.

In this tour we apprehended four deserters from Otway's regiment, who were going to the enemy, and whom I sent back to Fort Edward, with a part of my detachment, under the command of Lieutenant Stark, and proceeded with the remainder to compleat my orders, after which I returned to Saratoga to make my report.

There I met my brother Capt. Richard Rogers with his company, he being ordered back from Mohock river, to join me with the remainder of the Stockbridge Indians; and I marched both companies to Fort Edward, where I was ordered to form an encampment. A part of the Indian company were sent out on the east-side of Lake Champlain to alarm the enemy at Ticonderoga, whilst I, with a detachment of my own, and Capt. Richard Rogers's company, was ordered on another party down Lake George, in whale-boats, and the remainder of the companies were employed in reconnoitering round the encampment, and also served as flankers to the parties that guarded provisions to Lake George.

Capt. Jacob, who commanded the Indian party before-mentioned, returned two days before me with four French scalps, which they took opposite to Ticonderoga on the east-side.

September 7, 1756

Agreeable to orders, I this day embarked on Lake George, with a party of fourteen men in a whale-boat, which we laned, and concealed the evening following, on the east-shore, about four miles south of the French advance guard.

Here I divided my party, taking seven men with me, leaving the remainder in the charge of Mr. Chalmer (a volunteer sent me by Sir John Sinclair) with orders, upon his discovering the enemy's boats going up the lake, &c. to make the best of his way with the intelligence to Fort William-Henry.

I was the 9th current within half a mile of Ticonderoga fort, where I endeavoured to reconnoitre the enemy's works and strength. They were engaged in raising the walls of the fort, and had erected a large block-house near the south-east corner of the fort, with ports in it for cannon. East from the block-house was a battery, which I imagined commanded the lake. I discovered five houses south of the fort close to the water-side, and 160 tents south-west of the fort, and twenty-seven battoes hauled upon the beach.

Next morning, with one private, I went to view the falls betwixt Lake Champlain and Lake George (where I had heard the explosion of several guns the evening before, and had at that time sent Serjeant Henry to discover the reason of it) leaving the remainder of my party in charge of Mr. Gibbs, another volunteer, to wait our return.

Serjeant Henry followed soon after me, and reported, "that the French were building a small fort at the head of the falls on the east-side of the lake; that he also discovered their guard to the westward, and imagined both consisted of 500 men."

I returned, after finding the French were engaged in

building a saw-mill at the lower end of the falls, and found my boats with provisions left, as I suppose, by Mr. Chalmer and his party, whom I waited for till seven o'clock next day; but he not returning, and I judging from their tracks that they were returned to Fort William-Henry, we likewise began our return, and arrived safe the 11th of September, where I found Mr.Chalmer and the party left with him, he having punctually obeyed the orders given him above.

Upon my return, I communicated my observations upon the Lakes George and Champlain to my Lord Loudoun, giving him as just a description as I could of their situation.

September 24, 1756

General Abercrombie issued out orders, that three commissioned officers of the Rangers, with 20 privates each, should reconnoitre the Wood Creek, South Bay, and Ticonderoga; and these were alternately sent out, so that a continual scout was kept up for a considerable time.

October 22, 1756

The greatest part of the army was now at Fort-Edward, under the command of General Abercrombie, and Lord Loudoun arriving about this time with the remainder, it was generally expected that the army would cross the lake, and endeavour to reduce the French forts, notwithstanding the season was so far advanced; but his Lordship taking into consideration the probability that those lakes would freeze (which they generally do in the month of December) in which case no supplies could be had from, nor any communication kept up with Fort William-Henry; he determined to desist from this design, and contented himself with keeping the field till Mons. Montcalm retired to winter-quarters, and accordingly sought all opportunities to learn his situation and movements.

Agreeable to orders from his Lordship, I this day embarked in two whale-boats, with a party of twenty men, upon Lake George with an intent to bring a prisoner from Ticonderoga.

We passed the Narrows twenty miles from our embarkation, when Capt. Shephard (who was made a captive in August last and carried to Canada) hailed our boat; I knew his voice, and took him on board with three other men, one of whom was taken with him. He reported, that he left Canada fifteen days before.

I went on my course till the 27th, towards Carillon, and landed that night on the west-side of the lake, concealed our boats, and travelled by land to within a mile of the fort.

I kept spies out the day after to improve any opportunity that might offer, and the next day sent them still nearer, but to no good purpose; I at length discovered two men, centries to the piquet guard of the French Army, one of which was posted on the road that leads from the fort to the woods: I took five of my party, and marched directly down the road in the middle of the day, till we were challenged by a centry. I answered in French, signifying that we were friends; the centinel was thereby deceived, till I came close to him, when perceiving his mistake, in great surprize he called, Qui etes vous? I answered, Rogers, and led him from his post in great haste, cutting his breeches and coat from him, that he might march with greater ease and expedition.

With this prisoner we arrived at Fort William-Henry, Oct. 31, 1756.

Upon examination, he reported, "That he belonged to the regiment Languedoc: that he left Brest last April was a twelve-month, and had served since at Lake Champlain, Crown Point, and Carillon, was last year with General Dieskaw in the battle at Fort William-Henry: that they lost in that engagement of regulars, Canadians, and Indians, a great number: that at Carillon were at this time mounted thirty-six pieces of cannon, viz. twelve eighteen pounders, fifteen twelve pounders, and eight nine pounders: that at Crown Point were eighteen pieces, the largest of which were eighteen pounders: that Mons. Montcalm's forces this year at Carillon were 3000 regulars, and 2000 Canadians and Indians: that Montcalm himself was drawn off with one battalion, and that the forces then in that neighbourhood consisted of five battalions and about 800 Canadians: that the Indians were all gone off, 200 of whom talked of returning to spend the winter at Carillon: that the advanced guard on the west-side above the falls were all drawn in, and that that on the east consisted of 600 men, who were to decamp the 1st of November: that they had a camp of five battalions, and sixty Canadians, about half a league from Carillon, and that the rest of the army were under the fort: that they had barracks sufficient for 500 men, which he understood were to quarter there: that they had one schooner and 200 battoes on Lake Champlain, and but five or six on

Lake George: that Mons. the Chevalier de Levi commanded in Mons. Montcalm's absence, and that the Canadians were commanded by Messieurs le Corn and Columbie: that when Monsieur Montcalm went off, he said he had done enough for this year, and would take Fort William-Henry early in the spring: that the French had taken four of Captain Rogers's whale-boats in Lake Champlain: that when he was taken prisoner, he imagined himself to be about a gun-shot and a half from the fort, and that the French camp was pretty healthy."

From this time we were constantly employed in patrolling the woods about Fort Edward till the 19th of November 1756, when I had his Lordship's orders to take another excursion down the Lake. Captain Abercrombie, Aid-de-camp and nephew to General Abercrombie, did me the honour to accompany me; but nothing material being in our power to effect, except taking a view of the fort and works of the enemy at Ticonderoga, we returned safe to Fort Edward the 25th in the evening.

About this time his Lordship drew off the main body of the troops from Fort Edward to be quartered at Albany and New York.

Both armies being now retired to winter-quarters, nothing material happened to the end of this year. The Rangers were stationed at the Forts William-Henry and Edward, to which also two new companies of Rangers were sent this fall, commanded by Captain Spikeman and Captain Hobbs, in one of which my brother James Rogers was appointed an Ensign.

These two companies were stationed at Fort William-Henry mine and my brother Richard's at Fort Edward.

Captain Richard Rogers had leave to go into New England for recruits to complete our two companies. He this winter waited upon the government of Boston, to obtain pay for our services in the winter of 1755 before-mentioned, but could obtain none, notwithstanding Lord Loudoun, who was then at Boston, generously supported and enforced our solicitations with his interest.

January 15, 1757

Agreeable to orders from the commanding officer at Fort Edward, I this day marched with my own Lieutenant Mr. Stark, Ensign Page of Captain Richard Rogers's company, and fifty privates of said companies, to Fort William-Henry, where we were employed in providing provisions, snow-shoes, &c. till the 17th, when being joined by Captain Spikeman, Lieutenant Kennedy and Ensign Brewer of his company, and fourteen of their men, together with Ensign James Rogers and fourteen men of Captain Hobbs's company, and Mr. Baker, a volunteer of the 44th regiment of foot, we began our march on the ice down Lake George, and at night encamped on the east-side of the First Narrows.

The next morning, finding that some of the detachment had hurt themselves in the march the day before, as many were dismissed to return to the fort, as reduced our party to seventy-four men, officers included.

The 18th we marched twelve miles down the lake, and encamped on the west-side of it.

The 19th we marched three miles from our encampment further down the lake, and then took the land, and, upon snow-shoes, travelled north-west about eight miles from our landing, and three from the lake, where we encamped.

The 20th we marched north-by-east the whole day, and at night encamped on the western-side, opposite to and about three miles distant from Lake Champlain.

The 21st we marched east, till we came to the lake, about mid-way between Crown Point and Ticonderoga, and immediately discovered a sled going from the latter to the former. I ordered Lieutenant Stark, with twenty men, to head the sled, while I, with a party, marched the other way to prevent its retreating back again, leaving Captain Spikeman in the center with the remainder.

I soon discovered eight or ten sleds more following down the lake, and endeavoured to give Mr. Stark intelligence of it before he sallied on the lake and discovered himself to them, but could not. They all hastily returned towards Ticonderoga. We pursued them, and took seven prisoners, three sleds, and six horses; the remainder made their escape.

We examined the captives separately, who reported, "That 200 Canadians and 45 Indians were just arrived at Ticonderoga, and were to be reinforced that evening, by fifty Indians more from Crown Point: that there were 600 regular troops at that fortress, and 350 at Ticonderoga, where they soon expected a large number of troops, who in the spring were to besiege our forts: that they had large magazines of provisions in their forts, and that the above-mentioned party were well equipped, and in a condition to march upon any emergency at the least notice, and were designed soon to way-lay and distress our convoys between the forts."

From this account of things, and knowing that those who escaped would give early notice of us at Ticonderoga, I concluded it best to return; and ordered the party, with the utmost expedition, to march to the fires we had kindled the night before, and prepare for a battle, if it should be offered, by drying our guns, it being a rainy day, which we effected; and then marched in a single file, myself and Lieutenant Kennedy in the front Lieutenant Stark in the rear, and Captain Spikeman in the center. Ensigns Page and Rogers were between the front and center, and Ensign Brewer between center and rear, Serjeant Walker having command of a rear-guard.

In this manner we advanced half a mile, or thereabouts, over broken ground, when passing a valley of about fifteen rods breadth, the front having reached the summit of a hill on the west-side of it; the enemy, who had here drawn up in the form of a half-moon, with a design, as we supposed, to surround us, saluted us with a volley of about 200 shot, at the distance of about five yards from the nearest, or front, and thirty from the rear of their party.

This fire was about two o'clock in the afternoon, and proved fatal to Lieutenant Kennedy, and Mr. Gardner, a volunteer in my company, and wounded me and several others; myself, however, but lightly in the head.

We immediately returned their fire. I then ordered my men to the opposite hill, where I supposed Lieutenant Stark and Ensign Brewer had made a stand with forty men to cover us, in case we were obliged to retreat.

We were closely pursued, and Capt. Spikeman, with several of the party, were killed, and others made prisoners. My people, however, beat them back by a brisk fire from the hill, which gave us an opportunity to ascend, and post ourselves to advantage. After which I ordered Lieutenant Stark and Mr. Baker in the center, with Ensign Rogers; Serjeants Walter and Phillips, with a party, being a reserve, to prevent our being flanked, and watch the motions of the enemy.

Soon after we had thus formed ourselves for battle, the enemy attempted to flank us on the right, but the above reserve bravely attacked them, and giving them the first fire very briskly, it stopped several from retreating to the main body.

The enemy then pushed us closely in the front; but having the advantage of the ground, and being sheltered by large trees, we maintained a continual fire upon them, which killed several, and obliged the rest to retire to their main body. They then attempted to flank us again, but were again met by our reserved party, and repulsed. Mr. Baker about this time was killed. We maintained a pretty constant fire on both sides, till the darkness prevented our seeing each other, and about sun-set I received a ball thro' my hand and wrist, which

47

disabled me from loading my gun. I however found means to keep my people from being intimidated by this accident; they gallantly kept their advantageous situation, till the fire ceased on both sides.

The enemy, during this action, used many arts and stratagems to induce us to submit, sometimes threatening us with severity if we refused, assuring us that they every moment expected a large reinforcement, which should cut us to pieces without mercy: at other times flattering and cajolling us, declaring it was a pity so many brave men should be lost; that we should, upon our surrender, be treated with the greatest compassion and kindness; calling me by name, they gave me the strongest assurances of their esteem and friendship that words could do, but no one being dismayed by their menaces, or flattered by fair promises, we told them our numbers were sufficient, and that we were determined to keep our ground as long as there were two left to stand by each other.

After the action, in which we had a great number so severely wounded that they could not travel without assistance, and our ammunition being nearly expended, and considering that we were near to Ticonderoga, from whence the enemy might easily make a descent, and overpower us by numbers I thought it expedient to take the advantage of the night to retreat, and gave orders accordingly; and the next morning arrived at Lake George, about six miles south of the French advanced guard, from whence I dispatched Lieutenant Stark with two men to Fort William-Henry, to procure conveyances for our wounded men thither; and the next morning we were met by a party of fifteen men and a sled, under the command of Lieutenant Buckley, of Hobbs's company of Rangers, at the first narrows at Lake George.

Our whole party, which now consisted of only forty-eight effective, and six wounded men, arrived at Fort William-Henry the same evening, being the 23rd of January 1757.

The nearest computation we could make of the number

which attacked us, was, that it consisted of about 250 French and Indians; and we afterwards had an account from the enemy, that their loss in this action, of those killed, and who afterwards died of their wounds, amounted to 116 men.

Both the officers and soldiers I had the honour to command, who survived the first onset, behaved with the most undaunted bravery and resolution, and seemed to vie with each other in their respective stations who should excel.

Having laid this return before Major Sparks, commanding officer at Fort Edward, he transmitted the same to the General; and the 30th of January following, I wrote to Captain James Abercrombie, then at Albany, recommending such officers as I thought most deserving, to fill up the vacancies occasioned by our late action, among whom were Lieutenant Stark to be Captain of Spikeman's company, and Serjeant Joshua Martin to be Ensign in Captain Richard Rogers's company; and I also mentioned several things in favour of the Rangers. In consequence whereof I received the following answer.

Albany, Feb. 6, 1757.

DEAR SIR,

The General received your letter that was sent by Major Sparks, and returns you and your men thanks for their behaviour, and has recommended both you and them strongly to my Lord Loudoun, as also that they have payment for the prisoners they took. Upon receiving an account of your skirmish we sent an express to Boston, and, by the said opportunity, recommended, for Spikeman's company, your brother* for a Lieutenant. We expect the express back in a day or two, by whom, I dare say, we shall have my Lord's approbation of the Rangers. Please to send me the names of the officers you would recommend for your own company, and also to fill up the vacancies in the others; as I am certain you have

*James Rogers

49

The following is the RETURN which was made of the Killed, Wounded, and Missing, in the above action, viz.

Captain Rogers's Company.	Capt. Robert Rogers	—	—	Wounded
	Mr. Baker, Volunteer	Killed	—	—
	Mr. Gardner, ditto	ditto	—	—
	Thomas Henson	ditto	—	—
	Serjeant Martin	—	—	ditto
	Thomas Burnside	—	—	ditto
	Serjeant Henry	—	Missing	—
	William Morris	—	ditto	—
	John Morrison	—	ditto	—
C. Rd Rogers's do	Joseph Stephens	ditto	—	—
	Benjamin Woodall	—	ditto	—
	David Kemble	—	ditto	—
	Ensign Caleb Page	ditto	—	—
	David Page	—	—	ditto
Capt. Hobbs's ditto	Serjeant Jon Howard	ditto	—	—
	Phineas Kemp	ditto	—	—
	John Edmonds	ditto	—	—
	Thomas Farmer	ditto	—	—
	Emanuel Lapartaquer	ditto	—	—
Capt. Spikeman's ditto	Capt. Spikeman	ditto	—	—
	Lieut. Kennedy	ditto	—	—
	Robert Avery	ditto	—	—
	Thomas Brown	—	ditto	—
	Samuel Fisk	ditto	—	—
	Serjeant Moore	—	—	ditto
	John Caball	—	—	ditto
Total		14	6	6

N.B. *Those returned as missing, we afterwards found, had been taken prisoners by the enemy.*

the good of the service at heart, your recommendation will be paid great regard to. I yesterday received your's of the 30th January. You cannot imagine how all ranks of people here are pleased with your conduct, and your mens behaviour; for my part, it is no more than expected: I was so pleased with their appearance when I was out with them, that I took it for granted they would behave well whenever they met the enemy. When I returned I reported them as such, and am glad they have answered my expectation.

I am heartily sorry for Spikeman and Kennedy, who I imagined would have turned out well, as likewise for the men you have lost; but it is impossible to play at bowls without meeting with rubs. We must try to revenge the loss of them. There is few people that will believe it; but, upon honour, I could be glad to have been with you, that I might have learned the manner of fighting in this country. The chance of being shot is all stuff, and King William's opinion and principle is much the best for a soldier, viz. "that every bullet has its billet" and that "it is allotted how every man shall die;" so that I am certain that every one will agree, that it is better to die with the reputation of a brave man, fighting for his country in a good cause, than either shamefully running away to preserve one's life, or lingering out an old age, and dying in one's bed, without having done his country or his King any service.

The histories of this country, particularly, are full of the unheard-of cruelties committed by the French, and the Indians, by their instigation, which I think every brave man ought to do his utmost to humble that haughty nation, or reduce their bounds of conquest in this country to a narrow limit. As soon as General Abercrombie receives my Lord's instructions in regard to the Rangers, I shall send you notice of it; in the interim,

I hope you'll get the better of your wound. If I can be of any service to you or your men as long as they continue to behave so well, you may command.

Your most humble servant,

To Capt.   James Abercrombie,
Robert Rogers.   Aid de Camp.

My wound growing worse, I was obliged to repair to Albany for better assistance, and there received the following instructions from General Abercrombie, viz.

Instructions for Capt. ROBERT ROGERS

His Excellency the Earl of Loudoun having given authority to me to augment the company of Rangers under your command, to 100 men each, viz.

One Captain Two Lieutenants One Ensign	upon an English pay;
Four serjeants at 4s. each, New York currency;	
100 private men, at 2s. and 6d. each ditto per day;	

And whereas there are some private men of your company serving at present upon higher pay than the above establishment, you are at liberty to discharge them, in case they refuse to serve at the said establishment, as soon as you have other men to replace them. If your men agree to remain with you and serve upon the above establishment, you may assure them they will be taken notice of, and be first provided for; each man to be allowed ten dollars bounty-money, and to find their own cloaths, arms, and blankets, and to sign a paper subjecting themselves to the rules and articles of war, and to serve during the war. You are to inlist no vagrants, but such as you and your officers are acquainted with, and who are every way qualified for the duty of the Rangers; and you and your officers are to use your best endeavours to complete your companies as soon as possible, and bring them to Fort Edward.

James Abercrombie,
Major General.

About this time I again wrote to his Lordship, earnestly soliciting his friendly interposition and assistance, to obtain from the government here, an order for payment of what was due to me and my men, for our respective services during the winter 1755; but if that could not be obtained, that he would be pleased to direct me what method to take for recovery thereof. Whereto his Lordship replied, that as these services were antecedent to his command here, it was not in his power to reward them. General Amherst, afterwards, on a like application, gave me much the same answer.

These applications not being attended with any success, and suits of law being afterwards commenced against me, by, and on the behalf of those who served under me in that campaign, and verdicts obtained in their favour, I was not only obliged to answer their several demands, to the amount of £828:3:3 sterling, which I paid out of my private fortune; but also a considerable sum for law-charges, exclusive of what I ought to have received for my own services during that severe season. But for all which I have not at any time since received one shilling consideration.

In the same letter I likewise informed his Lordship of the death of Capt. Hobbs of the Rangers who died a few days before, and recommended Lieutenant Bulkley of the same company, as a proper person to succeed him in that command.

March 5, I was taken ill with the small-pox, and not able to leave my room till the 15th of April following, during which time my officers were recruiting, agreeable to his Lordship's instructions. Not long after I received the following letter from Capt. Abercrombie.

53

SIR,

As there is another ranging company sent up to Albany, with orders to procede to the forts, you will acquaint Colonel Gage, that it is my Lord Loudoun's orders, that the two companies at Fort William-Henry, and your own from Fort Edward, come down immediately to Albany, to be ready to embark for this place. Shew this letter to Colonel Gage, that he may acquaint Colonel Monro of his Lordship's orders, and that quarters may be provided for your companies in the houses about Albany. You will take particular care that the companies have provided themselves with all neccessaries, and see that they are complete and good men. Since his Lordship has put it in your charge, I hope you will be very dilligent in executing the trust, for, upon a review of the men, if any are found insufficient for the service, the blame will be laid upon you. If the officers of this ranging company that is gone up, are not acquainted with the woods about Fort William-Henry, your brother must send some officers and men of his company along with them, to let them know the different scouts. I am, Sir,

Your most humble servant,

To Capt.   James Abercrombie,
Robert Rogers,   Aid de Camp.
at Albany.

Capt. Richard Rogers, with his own, and the new company of Rangers before-mentioned, which was raised in the Jersies, and commanded by Capt. Burgin, being left at Fort William-Henry, my own company from Fort Edward, and Capt. Stark's and Capt. Bulkley's from Fort William-Henry, agreeable to the above instructions, marched down to Albany, and from thence embarked for New York, where we were joined by another new-raised company of Rangers, under command of Capt. Shephard from New Hampshire, and after some small stay there, re embarked on board a transport, and left Sandy Hook on the 20th of June, with a fleet of near an hundred sail, bound to Halifax, where we soon arrived, and, according to orders, I encamped on the Dartmouth-side of the harbour, while the army lay encamped on the Halifax-side. The Rangers were here employed in various services.

On July 3d, by orders, I commanded a party to Lawrence Town, and from thence to Schitzcook; some were left there to cut and make up hay in the meadows, for the horses intended to be used in an expedition to Loiusburg; others covered the hay-makers, and others were dispatched on scouts, to make discoveries; in one of which two deserters from the 45th regiment were seized and brought in.

About the latter end of this month forty Rangers were sent across the isthmus of Nova Scotia, to the settlements on the Bay of Fundy, and a party down to the north-west arm, to scour the woods for deserters, &c. and brought in several, both from the army and navy.

About this time Admiral Holborn arrived with a fleet from England, with several regiments of regular troops on board, which were landed, and likewise encamped at Halifax, upon which all scouting parties were called in; but certain intelligence being received that a French fleet of superior force had actually arrived at Louisburg, the intended expedition against that place was laid aside, and thereupon the Rangers were remanded back to the western frontiers.

Great numbers of the Rangers having been carried off this summer by the small-pox, I sent several of my officers, by his Lordship's command, to recruit in New Hampshire, and the Massachuset's provinces, with orders to join me at Albany. I afterwards embarked with the Rangers under my command, on board the fleet which carried the regular troops to New York, and from thence proceeded in small vessels up Hudson's

River to Albany, where I was soon after joined by the new-raised recruits.

I then proceeded to Fort Edward, which was the only remaining cover to the northern frontiers of New York, and the more eastern provinces, Fort William-Henry* having been taken by the French, under the command of Monsieur Montcalm, the August before. General Webb was then commanding officer at Fort Edward; and by his orders we were continually employed in patrolling the woods between this fort and Ticonderoga. In one of these parties, my Lord How did us the honour to accompany us, being fond, as he expressed himself, to learn our method of marching, ambushing, retreating, &c. and, upon our return, expressed his good opinion of us very generously.

About this time Lord Loudoun sent the following volunteers in the regular troops, to be trained to the ranging, or wood-service, under my command and inspection; with particular orders to me to instruct them to the utmost of my power in the ranging-discipline, our methods of marching, retreating, ambushing, fighting, &c. that they might be the better qualified for any future services against the enemy we had to contend with, desiring me to take particular notice of each one's behaviour, and to recommend them according to their several deserts, viz.

*My brother Captain Richard Rogers died with the small-pox a few days before this fort was besieged; but such was the cruelty and rage of the enemy after their conquest, that they dug him up out of his grave, and scalped him. In consequence of the articles of capitulation at the surrender of this fort, the two companies of Rangers there were disbanded, and dismissed the service.)

Walter Crofton Mr. Lyshat Mr. Roberts	of the 4th regiment of foot.
Charles Humbles Richard Edlington Andrew Crawley Thomas Millet	of the 22nd ditto.
John Wilcox John Wrighton Michael Kent Mr. Monsel Francis Creed	of the 27th ditto.
Alexander Robertson William Frazier John Graham Andrew Ross William Frazier, jun. Archibald Campbell Arch. Campbell, jun. Charles Menzies John Robertson	of the 42nd ditto.
Will. Ervin, or Irwin Thomas Drought William Drought Francis Carruthers John Clarke	of the 44th ditto.
Walter Paterson Mr. Nicholson Richard Boyce Charles Perry	of the 48th ditto.
Mr. Christopher Mr. Still Mr. Hamilton Mr. Young	of the 55th ditto.

Allen Grant Jonathon McDougal Mr. Frisborough	of the second battalion of Royal Americans
Nicholas Ward James Hill	of the 3rd ditto.
John Schloser George Wardoman Francis Barnard Engelbertus Horst Ericke Reinhault Andrew Wackerberg Luhainsans Dekesar Donald McBean Henry Ven Bebber John Boujour	of the 4th ditto.
Edward Crafton James Pottinger Simon Stephens Archibald McDonald Hugh Sterling Mr. Bridge	Rangers.

These volunteers I formed into a company by themselves, and took the more immediate command and management of them to myself; and for their benefit and instruction reduced into writing the following rules or plan of discipline, which, on various occasions, I had found by experience to be necessary and advantageous, viz.

I

All Rangers are to be subject to the rules and articles of war; to appear at roll-call every evening on their own parade, equipped, each with a fire-lock, sixty rounds of powder and ball, and a hatchet, at which time an officer from each company is to inspect the same, to see they are in order, so as to be ready on any emergency to march at a minute's warning; and before they are dismissed the neccessary guards are to be draughted, and scouts for the next day appointed.

II

Whenever you are ordered out to the enemies forts or frontiers for discoveries, if your number be small, march in single file, keeping at such distance from each other as to prevent one shot from killing two men, sending one man, or more, forward, and the like on each side, at the distance of twenty yards from the main body, if the ground you march over will admit of it, to give the signal to the officer of the approach of an enemy, and of their number, &c.

III

If you march over marshes or soft ground, change your position, and march abreast of each other, to prevent the enemy from tracking you, (as they would do if you marched in a single file) till you get over such ground, and then resume your former order, and march till it is quite dark before you encamp, which do, if possible, on a piece of ground that may afford your centries the advantage of seeing or hearing the enemy at some considerable distance, keeping one half of your whole party awake alternately through the night.

IV

Some time before you come to the place you would reconnoitre, make a stand, and send one or two men, in whom you can confide, to look out the best ground for making your observations.

V

If you have the good fortune to take any prisoners, keep them separate, till they are examined, and in your return take a different rout from that in which you went out, that you may the better discover any party in your rear, and have an opportunity, if their strength be superior to yours, to alter your course, or disperse, as circumstances may require.

VI

If you march in a large body of three or four hundred, with a design to attack the enemy, divide your party into three columns, each headed by a proper officer, and let these columns march in single files, the columns to the right and left keeping at twenty yards distance or more from that of the center, if the ground will admit, and let proper guards be kept in the front and rear, and suitable flanking parties at a due distance as before directed, with orders to halt on all eminences, to take a view of the surrounding ground, to prevent your being ambuscaded, and to notify the approach or retreat of the enemy, that proper dispositions may be made for attacking, defending, &c. And if the enemy approach in your front on level ground, form a front of your three columns or main body with the advanced guard, keeping your flanking parties, as if you were marching under the command of trusty officers, to prevent the enemy from pressing hard on either of your wings, or surrounding you, which is the usual method of the savages, if their number will admit of it, and be careful likewise to support and strengthen your rear-guard.

VII

If you are obliged to receive the enemy's fire, fall, or squat down, till it is over, then rise and discharge at them. If their main body is equal to yours, extend yourselves occasionally; but if superior, be careful to support and strengthen your flanking parties, to make them equal with theirs, that if possible you may repulse them to their main body, in which case push upon them with the greatest resolution, with equal force in each flank and in the center, observing to keep at a due distance from each other, and advance from tree to tree, with one half of the party before the other ten or twelve yards. If the enemy push upon you, let your front fire and fall down, and then let your rear advance thro' them and do the like, by which time those who before were in front will be ready to discharge again, and repeat the same alternately, as occasion shall require; by this means you will keep up such a constant fire, that the enemy will not be able easily to break your order, or gain your ground.

VIII

If you oblige the enemy to retreat, be careful, in your pursuit of them, to keep out your flanking parties, and prevent them from gaining eminences, or rising grounds, in which case they would perhaps be able to rally and repulse you in their turn.

IX

If you are obliged to retreat, let the front of your whole party fire and fall back, till the rear hath done the same, making for the best ground you can; by this means you will oblige the enemy to pursue you, if they do it at all, in the face of a constant fire.

X

If the enemy is so superior that you are in danger of being surrounded by them, let the whole body disperse, and every one take a different road to the place of rendezvous appointed for that evening, which must every morning be altered and fixed for the evening ensuing, in order to bring the whole party, or as many of them as possible, together, after any separation that may happen in the day; but if you should happen to be actually surrounded, form yourselves into a square, or if in the woods, a circle is best, and, if possible, make a stand till the darkness of the night favours your escape.

XI

If your rear is attacked, the main body and flankers must face about to the right or left, as occasion shall require, and form themselves to oppose the enemy, as before directed; and the same method must be observed, if attacked in either of your flanks, by which means you will always make a rear of one of your flank guards.

XII

If you determine to rally after a retreat, in order to make a fresh stand against the enemy, by all means endeavour to do it on the most rising ground you can come at, which will give you greatly the advantage in point of situation, and enable you to repulse superior numbers.

XIII

In general, when pushed upon by the enemy, reserve your fire till they approach very near, which will then put them into the greater surprize and consternation, and give you an opportunity of rushing upon them with your hatchets and cutlasses to the better advantage.

XIV

When you encamp at night, fix your centries in such a manner as not to be relieved from the main body till morning, profound secrecy and silence being often of the last importance in these cases. Each centry, therefore, should consist of six men, two of whom must be constantly alert, and when relieved by their fellows, it should be done without noise; and in case those on duty see or hear any thing, which alarms them, they are not to speak, but one of them is silently to retreat, and acquaint the commanding officer thereof, that proper dispositions may be made; and all occasional centries should be fixed in like manner.

XV

At the first dawn of day, awake your whole detachment;

that being the time when the savages chuse to fall upon their enemies, you should by all means be in readiness to receive them.

XVI

If the enemy should be discovered by your detachments in the morning, and their numbers are superior to yours, and a victory doubtful, you should not attack them till the evening, as then they will not know your numbers, and if you are repulsed, your retreat will be favoured by the darkness of night.

XVII

Before you leave your encampment, send out small parties to scout round it, to see if there be any appearance or track of an enemy that might have been near you during the night.

XVIII

When you stop for refreshment, chuse some spring or rivulet if you can, and dispose your party so as not to be surprised, posting proper guards and centries at a due distance, and let a small party waylay the path you came in, lest the enemy should be pursuing.

XIX

If, in your return, you have to cross rivers, avoid the usual fords as much as possible, lest the enemy should have discovered, and be there expecting you.

XX

If you have to pass by lakes, keep at some distance from the edge of the water, lest, in case of an ambuscade, or an attack from the enemy, when in that situation, your retreat should be cut off.

XXI

If the enemy pursue your rear, take a circle till you come

to your own tracks, and there form an ambush to receive them, and give them the first fire.

XXII

When you return from a scout, and come near our forts, avoid the usual roads, and avenues thereto, lest the enemy should have headed you, and lay in ambush to receive you, when almost exhausted with fatigues.

XXIII

When you pursue any party that has been near our forts or encampments, follow not directly in their tracks, lest you should be discovered by their rear-guards, who, at such a time, would be most alert; but endeavour, by a different route, to head and meet them in some narrow pass, or lay in ambush to receive them when and where they least expect it.

XXIV

If you are to embark in canoes, battoes, or otherwise,by water, chuse the evening for the time of your embarkation, as you will then have the whole night before you, to pass undiscovered by any parties of the enemy, on hills, or other places, which command a prospect of the lake or river you are upon.

XXV

In padling or rowing, give orders that the boat or canoe next the strernmost, wait for her, and the third for the second, and the fourth for the third, and so on, to prevent separation, and that you may be ready to assist each other on any emergency.

XXVI

Appoint one man in each boat to look out for fires, on the adjacent shores, from the numbers and size of which you may form some judgment of the number that kindled them, and whether you are able to attack them or not.

XXVII

If you find the enemy encamped near the banks of a river, or lake, which you imagine they will attempt to cross for their security upon being attacked, leave a detachment of your party on the opposite shore to receive them, while, with the remainder, you surprize them, having them between you and the lake or river.

XXVIII

If you cannot satisfy yourself as to the enemy's number and strength, from their fire, &c. conceal your boats at some distance, and ascertain their number by a reconnoitring party, when they embark, or march, in the morning, marking the course they steer, &c. when you may pursue, ambush, and attack them, or let them pass, as prudence shall direct you. In general, however, that you may not be discovered by the enemy on the lakes and rivers at a great distance, it is safest to lay by, with your boats and party concealed all day, without noise or shew, and to pursue your intended route by night; and whether you go by land or water, give out parole or countersigns, in order to know one another in the dark, and likewise appoint a station for every man to repair to, in case of any accident that may separate you.

Such in general are the rules to be observed in the Ranging service; there are, however, a thousand occurrences and circumstances which may happen, that will make it neccessary, in some measure, to depart from them, and to put other arts and stratagems in practice; in which cases every man's reason and judgment must be his guide, according to the particular situation and nature of things; and that he may do this to advantage, he should keep in mind a maxim never to be departed from by a commander, viz. to preserve a firmness and presence of mind on every occasion.

My Lord Loudoun about this time made a visit to Fort

Edward, and after giving directions for quartering the army the approaching winter, left a strong garrison there under the command of Colonel Haviland, and returned to Albany.

The Rangers*, with the before-mentioned volunteers, were encamped and quartered in huts on an adjacent island in Hudson's River, were sent out on various scouts, in which my ill state of health at this time would not permit me to accompany them, till December 17, 1757, when, pursuant to orders from Lieutenant Colonel Haviland, commanding officer at Fort Edward, I marched from thence with a party of 150 men to reconnoitre Carillon, alias Ticonderoga, and if possible to take a prisoner. We marched six miles and encamped, the snow being then about three inches deep, and before morning it was fifteen: we however pursued our route.

On the 18th in the morning, eight of my party being tired, returned to the fort; with the remainder I marched nine miles further, and encamped on the east-side of Lake George, near the place where Mons. Montcalm landed his troops when he besieged and took Fort William-Henry, where I found some cannon-ball and shells, which had been hid by the French, and made a mark by which I might find them again.

The 19th we continued our march on the west-side of the lake nine miles further, near the head of the north-west bay.

The 21st, so many of my party tired and returned as reduced our number to 123, officers included, with whom I proceeded ten miles further, and encamped at night, ordering each man to leave a day's provisions there till our return.

The next day we marched ten miles further, and encamped near the great brook that runs into Lake George, eight miles from the French advanced guard.

The 23rd we marched eight miles, and the 24th six more, and then halted within 600 yards of Carillon Fort. Near the

*Several of them were dismissed with an allowance of thirteen days pay to carry them home, being rendered unfit for immediate service by their past fatigues, and several officers were sent recruiting in order to have the companies complete by the opening of the spring.

mills we discovered five Indian's tracks, that had marched that way the day before, as we supposed, on a hunting party. On my march this day between the advanced guard and the fort, I appointed three places of rendezvous to repair to, in case of being broke in an action, and acquainted every officer and soldier that I should rally the party at the nearest post to the fort, and it broke there to retreat to the second, and at the third to make a stand till the darkness of the night would give us an opportunity to get off. Soon after I halted, I formed an ambush on a road leading from the fort to the woods, with an advanced party of twenty men, and a rear-guard of fifteen.

About eleven o'clock a serjeant of marines came from the fort up the road to my advanced party, who let him pass to the main body, where I made him prisoner. Upon examination, he reported, "that there were in the garrison 350 regulars, about fifty workmen, and about five Indians: that they had plenty of provisions, &c. and that twelve masons were constantly employed in blowing up rocks in the entrenchment, and a number of soldiers to assist them: that at Crown Point there were 150 soldiers and fourteen Indians: that Mons. Montcalm was at Montreal: that 500 Ottawawas Indians wintered in Canada, and that 500 Rangers were lately raised in Canada, each man having a double-barrelled fuzee, and put under an experienced officer, well acquainted with the country: that he did not know whether the French intended to attack any of the English forts this winter or not; but that they expected a great number of Indians as soon as the ice would bear them, in order to go down to the English forts; and that all the bakers in Carillon were employed in baking biscuit for the scouts above-mentioned."

About noon, a Frenchman, who had been hunting, came near my party in his return, when I ordered a party to pursue him to the edge of the cleared ground, and take him prisoner, with this caution, to shoot off a gun or two, and then retreat to the main body, in order to intice the enemy from their fort;

which orders were punctually obeyed, but not one of them ventured out.

The last prisoner, on examination, gave much the same account as the other, but with this addition, "that he had heard the English intended to attack Ticonderoga, as soon as the lake was froze so as to bear them."

When I found the French would not come out of the fort, we went about killing their cattle, and destroyed seventeen head, and set fire to the wood, which they had collected for the use of the garrison, and consumed five large piles; the French shot off some cannon at the fires, but did us no harm.

At eight o'clock at night I began my march homewards, and arrived at Fort Edward with my prisoners the 27th. In my return, I found at the north-end of Lake George, where the French had hid the boats they had taken at Fort William Henry, with a great number of cannon-balls; but as the boats were under water we could not destroy them.

Upon my return to Fort Edward, I received a letter from Captain Abercrombie, informing me that the Earl of Loudoun, who was then at New York, had thoughts of augmenting the Rangers, and had desired General Abercrombie to command me down to receive his directions. I accordingly prepared for my journey, and upon my arrival was received by his Lordship in a very friendly manner; and, after much conversation upon the subject, he was pleased to inform me of his intentions of levying five additional companies of Rangers, desiring me to name the persons whom I thought fit for officers, and such as might be depended upon, to levy the men his Lordship desired; which I accordingly did, and then received from him the following instructions.

By his Excellency John Earl of Loudoun, Lord Machline and Tairenseen &c. &c. &c. one of the sixteen peers of Scotland, Governor and Captain General of Virginia, and vice Admiral of the same, Colonel of the

13th Regiment of foot, Colonel in chief of the Royal American regiment, Major General and Commander in Chief of all his Majesty's forces, raised or to be raised in North America:

Whereas I have this day thought proper to augment the Rangers with five additional companies, that is, four New England and one Indian company, to be forthwith raised and employed in his Majesty's service; and whereas I have an entire confidence in your skill and knowledge, of the men most fit for that service; I do therefore, by these presents, appoint you to raise such a number of non-commissioned officers and private men as will be necessary to compleat the said five companies, upon the following establishment, viz. each company to consist of one Captain, two Lieutenants, one Ensign, four Serjeants, and 100 privates. The officers to have British pay, that is, the same as an officer of the line rank in his Majesty's regular forces; the Serjeants 4s. New York currency per day, and the private men 2s. 6d. currency per day. And the better to enable you to make this levy of men, you shall have one month's pay for each of the said five companies advanced to you; upon these conditions, that, out of these first warrants that shall hereafter be granted for the subsistence of these companies, shall be deducted the said month's pay, now advanced. Your men to find their own arms, which must be such as upon examination, shall be found fit, and be approved of. They are likewise to provide themselves with good warm cloathing, which must be uniform in every company, and likwise with good warm blankets, And, the company of Indians to be dressed in all respects in the true Indian fashion, and they are all to be subject to the rules and articles of war. You will forthwith acquaint the officers appointed to these companies, that they are immediately to set out on the recruiting service, and you will not fail to instruct them that they are not to inlist any man for less term than one year, nor any but what are able-bodied, well acquainted with the woods, used to hunting, and every way qualified for the Rangeing service. You are also to observe that the number of men requisite to compleat the said five companies, are all to be at Fort Edward on or before the 15th day of March next ensuing, and those that shall come by the way of Albany are to be mustered there by the officer commanding, as shall those who go strait to Fort Edward by the officer commanding there. Given under my hand, at New York, the 11th day of January 1758.

LOUDOUN.

By his Excellency's command,

To Capt.
Robert Rogers.   J. APPY.

In pursuance of the above instructions, I immediately sent officers into the New England provinces, where, by the assistance of my friends, the requested augmentation of Rangers was quickly compleated, the whole five companies being ready for service by the 4th day of March.

Four of these companies were sent to Louisburg to join General Amherst, and one joined the corps under my command; and tho' I was at the whole expence of raising the five companies, I never got the least allowance for it, and one of the Captain's dying, to whom I had delivered a thousand dollars as advance pay for his company, which, agreeable to the instructions I received, I had a right to do; yet was I obliged to account with the government for this money, and entirely lost every penny of it.

It has already been mentioned, that the garrison at Fort Edward was this winter under the command of Lieut. Col. Haviland. This gentleman, about the 28th of February, ordered out a scout under the direction of one Putnam, Captain of a company of one of the Connecticut provincial regiments, with some of my men, giving out publickly at the same time, that, upon Putnam's return, I should be sent to the French forts with a strong party of 400 Rangers. This was known not only to all the officers, but soldiers also, at Fort Edward before Putnam's departure.

While this party was out, a servant of Mr. Best, a sutler to the Rangers was captivated by a flying party of the enemy from Ticonderoga; unfortunately too, one of Putnam's men had left him at Lake George, and deserted to the enemy. Upon Captain Putnam's return, we were informed that he had ventured within eight miles of the French fort at Ticonderoga, and that a party he had sent to make discoveries had reported to him, that there were near 600 Indians not far from the enemy's quarters.

March 10, 1758

Soon after the said Captain Putnam's return, in consequence of positive orders from Col. Haviland, I this day began a march from Fort Edward for the neighbourhood of Carillon, not with a party of 400 men, as at first given out, but of 180 men only, officers included, one Captain, one Lieutenant, and one Ensign, and three volunteers, viz. Mess. Creed, Kent and Wrightson, one serjeant, and one private, all volunteers of the 27th regiment; and a detachment from the four companies of Rangers, quartered on the island near Fort Edward, viz. Capt. Bulkley, Lieutenants Philips, Moore, Crafton, Campbell, and Pottinger; Ensigns Ross, Wait, McDonald, and White, and 162 private men.

I acknowledge I entered upon this service, and viewed this small detachment of brave men march out, with no little concern and uneasiness of mind; for as there was the greatest reason to suspect, that the French were, by the prisoner and the deserter above mentioned, fully informed of the design of sending me out upon Putnam's return: what could I think! to see my party, instead of being strengthened and augmented, reduced to less than one half of the number at first proposed. I must confess it appeared to me (ignorant and unskilled as I then was in politicks and the arts of war) incomprehensible; *but my commander doubtless had his reasons*, and is able to vindicate his own conduct.

We marched to the half-way brook, in the road leading to Lake George, and there encamped the first night.

The 11th we proceeded as far as the first Narrows on Lake George, and encamped that evening on the east-side of the lake; and after dark, I sent a party three miles further down, to see if the enemy might be coming towards our forts, but they returned without discovering any. We were however on our guard, and kept parties walking on the lake all night, besides centries at all necessary places on the land.

The 12th we marched from our encampment at sun-rise, and having distanced it about three miles, I saw a dog running across the lake, whereupon I sent a detachment to reconnoitre the island, thinking the Indians might have laid in ambush there for us; but no such could be discovered; upon which I thought it expedient to put to shore, and lay by till night, to prevent any party from descrying us on the lake, from hills, or otherwise. We halted at a place called Sabbath-day Point, on the west-side of the lake, and sent out parties to look down the lake with perspective glasses, which we had for that purpose.

As soon as it was dark we proceeded down the lake. I sent Lieutenant Philips with fifteen men, as an advanced guard, some of whom went before him on scates, while Ensign Ross flanked us on the left under the west-shore, near which we kept the main body, marching as close as possible, to prevent separation, it being a very dark night. in this manner we continued our march till within eight miles of the French advanced guards, when Lieutenant Philips sent a man on scates back to me, to desire me to halt; upon which I ordered my men to squat down upon the ice.

Mr. Philips soon came to me himself, leaving his party to look out, and said, he imagined he had discovered a fire* on the east-shore, but was not certain; upon which I sent with him Ensign White, to make further discovery. In about an hour they returned, fully persuaded that a party of the enemy was encamped there. I then called in the advanced guard, and flanking party, and marched on to the west-shore, where, in a thicket, we hid our sleys and packs, leaving a small guard

*A small party of the French, as we have since heard, had a fire here at this time; but, discovering my advanced party, extinguished their fire, and carried the news of our approach to the French fort.

73

with them, and with the remainder I marched to attack the enemy's encampment, if there was any; but when we came near the place, no fires were to be seen, which made us conclude that we had mistaken some bleach patches of snow, or pieces of rotten wood, for fire (which in the night, at a distance, resembles it) whereupon we returned to our packs, and there lay the remainder of the night without fire.

The 13th, in the morning, I deliberated with the officers how to proceed, who were unanimously of opinion, that it was best to go by land in snow-shoes, lest the enemy should discover us on the lake; we accordingly continued our march on the west-side, keeping on the back of the mountains that overlooked the French advanced guards.

At twelve of the clock we halted two miles west of those guards, and there refreshed ourselves till three, that the day-scout from the fort might be returned home before we advanced; intending at night to ambuscade some of their roads, in order to trepan them in the morning. We then marched in two divisions, the one headed by Captain Bulkley, the other by myself: Ensigns White and Wait had the rear-guard, the other officers were posted properly in each division, having a rivulet at a small distance on our left; and a steep mountain on our right. We kept close to the mountain, that the advanced guard might better observe the rivulet, on the ice of which I imagined they would travel if out, as the snow was four feet deep, and very bad travelling on snow-shoes.

In this manner we marched a mile and an half, when our advanced guard informed me of the enemy being in their view; and soon after, that they had ascertained their number to be ninety-six, chiefly Indians.

We immediately laid down our packs, and prepared for battle, supposing these to be the whole number or main body of the enemy, who were marching on our left up the rivulet, upon the ice. I ordered Ensign McDonald to the command of the advanced guard, which, as we faced to the left, made a flanking party to our right. We marched to within a few yards of the bank, which was higher than the ground we occupied; and observing the ground gradually to descend from the bank of the rivulet to the foot of the mountain, we extended our party along the bank, far enough to command the whole of the enemy's at once; we waited till their front was nearly opposite to our left wing, when I fired a gun, as a signal for a general discharge upon them; whereupon we gave them the first fire, which killed above forty Indians; the rest retreated, and were pursued by about one half of our people.

I now imagined the enemy totally defeated, and ordered Ensign McDonald to head the flying remains of them, that none might escape; but we soon found our mistake, and that the party we had attacked were only their advanced guard, their main body coming up, consisted of 600 more, Canadians and Indians; upon which I ordered our people to retreat to their own ground, which we gained at the expence of fifty men killed; the remainder I rallied, and drew up in pretty good order, where they fought with such intrepidity and bravery as obliged the enemy (tho' seven to one in number) to retreat a second time; but we not being in a condition to pursue them, they rallied again, and recovered their ground, and warmly pushed us in front and both wings, while the mountain defended our rear; but they were so warmly received, that their flanking parties soon retreated to their main body with considerable loss.

This threw the whole again into disorder, and they retreated a third time; but our number being now too far reduced to take advantage of their disorder, they rallied again, and made a fresh attack upon us.

About this time we discovered 200 Indians going up the mountain on our right, as we supposed, to get possession of the rising ground, and attack our rear; to prevent which I sent Lieutenant Philips, with eighteen men, to gain the first possession, and beat them back; which he did: and being

75

suspicious that the enemy would go round on our left, and take possession of the other part of the hill, I sent Lieutenant Crafton, with fifteen men, to prevent them there; and soon after desired two gentlemen, who were volunteers in the party*, with a few men, to go and support him, which they did with great bravery.

The enemy pushed us so close in front, that the parties were not more than twenty yards asunder in general, and sometimes intermixed with each other. The fire continued almost constant for an hour and half from beginning of the attack, in which time we lost eight officers, and more than 100 private men killed on the spot.

We were at last obliged to break, and I with about twenty men ran up the hill to Philips and Crafton, where we stopped and fired on the Indians, who were eagerly pushing us, with numbers that we could not withstand.

Lieutenant Philips being surrounded by 300 Indians, was at this time capitulating for himself and party, on the other part of the hill. He spoke to me, and said if the enemy would give them good quarters, he thought it best to surrender, otherwise that he would fight while he had one man left to fire a gun**.

I now thought it most prudent to retreat, and bring off with me as many of my party as I possibly could, which I immediately did; the Indians closely pursuing us at the same time, took several prisoners. We came to Lake George in the evening, where we found several wounded men, whom we took

---

* I had before this desired these gentlemen to retire, offering them a serjeant to conduct them; that as they were not used to snow-shoes, and were quite unacquainted with the woods, they would have no chance of escaping the enemy, in case we should be broke and put to flight, which I very much suspected. They at first seemed to accept the offer, and began to retire; but seeing us so closely beset, they undauntedly returned to our assistance. What befel them after our flight, may be seen by a letter from one of the Gentlemen to the commanding officer, which I have inserted next to this account of our scout.

* *This unfortunate officer, and his whole party, after they surrendered, upon the strongest assurances of good treatment from the enemy, were inhumanly tied up to trees, and hewn to pieces, in a most barbarous and shocking manner.

with us to the place where we had left our sleds, from whence I sent an express to Fort Edward, desiring Mr. Haviland to send a party to meet us, and assist in bringing in the wounded; with the remainder I tarried there the whole night, without fire or blankets, and in the morning we proceeded up the lake, and met with Captain Stark at Hoop Island, six miles north from Fort William-Henry, and encamped there that night; the next day being the 15th, in the evening, we arrived at Fort Edward.

The number of the enemy was about 700, 600 of which were Indians. By the best account we could get, we killed 150 of them, and wounded as many more. I will not pretend to determine what we should have done had we been 400 or more strong; but this I am obliged to say of those brave men who attended me (most of whom are now no more) both officers and soldiers in their respective stations behaved with uncommon resolution and courage; nor do I know an instance during the whole action in which I can justly impeach the prudence or good conduct of any one of them.

The following is a LIST of the Killed, Missing, &c.

The Captain and Lieutenant of his Majesty's regular troops, volunteers in this party, were taken prisoners; the Ensign, another volunteer of the same corps, was killed, as were two volunteers, and a serjeant of the said corps, and one private.

Of Capt. Rogers's Company,

Lieut. Moore	Killed
Serjeant Parnell	Ditto
Thirty-six privates	Ditto

Of Capt. Shepherd's Company,
Two Serjeants
Sixteen Privates

Of Capt. James Rogers's Company,

Ensign McDonald	Killed

Of Capt. John Starks's Company,

Two Serjeants	Killed
Fourteen Privates	Ditto

Of Capt. Bulkley's Company,

Capt. Bulkley	Killed
Lieut. Pottinger	Ditto
Ensign White	Ditto
Forty-seven privates	K. and Miss.

Of Capt. William Starks's Company,

Ensign Ross	Killed

Of Capt. Brewer's Company

Lieut. Campbell	Killed

A Gentleman of the army, who was a volunteer on this party, and who with another fell into the hands of the French, wrote the following letter, some time after, to the officer commanding the regiment they belonged to at Fort Edward.

Carillon, March 28, 1758.

Dear Sir,

As a flag of truce is daily expected here with an answer to Monsieur Vaudreuil, I sit down to write the moment I am able, in order to have a letter ready, as no doubt you and our friends at Fort Edward are anxious to be informed about Mr. ———— and me, whom probably you have reckoned amongst the slain in our unfortunate rencontre of the 13th concerning which at present I shall not be particular; only to do this justice to those who lost their lives there, and to those who have escaped, to assure you, Sir, that such dispositions were made by the enemy, (who discovered us long enough before) it was impossible for a party so weak as ours to hope for even a retreat. Towards the conclusion of the affair, it was cried from a rising ground on our right, to retire there; where, after scrambling with difficulty, as I was unaccustomed to snow-shoes, I found Capt. Rogers, and told him, that I saw to retire further was impossible, therefore earnestly begged we might collect all the men left, and make a stand there. Mr. ———, who was with him, was of my opinion, and Capt. Rogers also; who therefore desired me to maintain one side of the hill, whilst he defended the other. Our parties did not exceed above ten or twelve in each, and mine was shifting towards the mountain, leaving me unable to defend my post, or to labour with them up the hill. In the mean time, Capt. Rogers with his party came to me, and said (as did all those with him) that a large body of Indians had ascended to our right; he likewise added, what was true, that the combat was very unequal, that I must retire, and he would give Mr. ——— and me a Serjeant to conduct us thro' the mountain. No doubt prudence required us to accept his offer; but, besides one of my snow-shoes being untied, I knew myself unable to march as fast as was requisite to avoid becoming a sacrifice to an enemy we could no longer oppose; I therefore begged him to proceed, and then leaned against a rock in the path, determined to submit to a fate I thought unavoidable. Unfortunately for Mr. ——— his snow-shoes were loosened likewise, which obliged him to determine with me, not to labour in a flight we were both unequal to. Every instant we expected the savages; but what induced them to quit this path, in which we actually saw them, we are ignorant of, unless they changed it for a shorter, to intercept those who had just left us. By their noise, and making a fire, we imagined they had got the rum in the Rangers packs. This thought, with the approach of night, gave us the first hopes of retiring; and when the moon arose we marched to the southward along the mountains about three hours, which brought us to ice, and gave us reason to hope our difficulties were almost past; but we knew not we had enemies yet to combat with, more cruel than the savages we had escaped. We marched all night, and on the morning of the 14th found ourselves entirely unacquainted with the ice. Here we saw a man, who came towards us; he was the servant of Capt. Rogers, with whom he had been oftentimes all over the country, and, without the least hesitation whatsoever, he informed us we were upon South-Bay; that Wood-Creek was just before us; that he knew the way to Fort Anne extremely well, and would take us to Fort Edward the next day. Notwithstanding we were disappointed in our hopes of being upon Lake George, we thought ourselves fortunate in meeting such a guide, to whom we gave entire confidence, and which he in fact confirmed, by bringing us to a creek, where he shewed the tracks of Indians, and the path he said they had taken to Fort Anne. After struggling thro' the snow some hours, we were obliged to halt to make snow-shoes, as Mr. ———— and the guide had left theirs at arriving upon the ice. Here we remained all night, without any blankets, no coat, and but a single waistcoat each, for I gave one of mine to Mr. ————, who had laid aside his green jacket in the field, as I did likewise my furred cap, which became a mark to the enemy, and probably was the cause of a slight wound in my face; so that I had but a silk handkerchief on my head, and our fire could not be large, as we had nothing to cut wood with. Before morning we contrived, with forked sticks and strings of leather, a sort of snow-shoes, to prevent sinking entirely; and, on the 15th, followed our guide west all day, but he did not fulfil his promise; however the next day it was impossible to fail: but even then, the 16th, he was unsuccessful; yet still we were patient, because he seemed well acquainted with the way, for he gave every mountain a name, and shewed us several places, where he said his master had either killed deer or encamped. The ground, or rather the want of sun-shine, made us incline to the southward, from whence by accident we saw ice, at several miles distance, to the south-east. I was very certain, that, after searching two days west of South Bay, Lake George could not lie south-east from us, and therefore concluded this to be the upper end of the bay we had left. For this reason, together with the assurances of our guide, I advised continuing our course to the west, which must shortly strike Fort Anne, or some other place that we knew. But Mr. —— wished to be upon ice at any rate; he was unable to continue in the snow, for the difficulties of our march had overcome him. And really, Sir, was I to be minute in those we had experienced already and afterwards, they would almost be as tiresome for you to read, as they were to us to suffer.

Our snow-shoes breaking, and sinking to our middle every fifty paces, the scrambling up mountains, and across fallen timber, our nights without sleep or covering, and but little fire, gathered with great fatigue, our sustenance mostly water and the bark and berries of trees; for all our provisions from the beginning was only a small Bologna sausage, and a little ginger, I happened to have, and which even now was very much decreased; so that I knew not how to oppose Mr. ——'s intreaties; but as our guide still persisted Fort Anne was near, we concluded to search a little longer, and if we made no discovery to proceed next day towards the ice; but we sought in vain, as did our guide the next morning, tho' he returned, confidently asserting he had discovered fresh proofs, that the fort could not be far off. I confess I was still inclined to follow him, for I was almost certain the best we could hope from descending upon this ice to our left, was to throw ourselves into the hands of the French, and perhaps not be able to effect even that; but, from the circumstances I have mentioned, it was a point I must yield to, which I did with great reluctancy. The whole day of the 17th we marched a dreadful road, between the mountains, with but one good snow-shoe each, the other of our own making being almost useless. The 18th brought us to the ice, which tho' we longed to arrive at, yet I still dreaded the consequence, and with reason, for the first sight informed us, it was the very place we had left five days before. Here I must own my resolution almost failed me; when fatigue, cold, hunger, and even the prospect of perishing in the woods attended us, I still had hopes, and still gave encouragement, but now I wanted it myself; we had no resource but to throw ourselves into the enemy's hands, or perish. We had nothing to eat, our slender stock had been equally shared amongst us three, and we were not so fortunate as ever to see either bird or beast to shoot at. When our first thoughts were a little calmed, we conceived hopes, that, if we appeared before the French fort, with a white flag, the commanding officer would relieve and return us to Fort Edward. This served to palliate our nearset approach to despair, and determined a resolution, where, in fact, we had no choice. I knew Carillon had an extensive view up South Bay, therefore we concluded to halt during the evening, and march in the night, that we might approach it in the morning, besides the wind pierced us like a sword; but instead of its abating it increased, together with a freezing rain, that incrusted us entirely with ice, and obliged us to remain until morning, the 19th, when we fortunately got some juniper berries, which revived, gave us spirits, and I thought strength. We were both so firmly of that opinion, that we proposed taking the advantage of its being a dark snowy day, to approach Carillon, to pass it in the night, and get upon Lake George. With difficulty we persuaded the guide to be of our opinion, we promised large rewards in vain, until I assured him of provisions hid upon the lake; but we little considered how much nature was exhausted, and how unequal we were to the task: however, a few miles convinced us we were soon midway up our legs in the new-fallen snow; it drove full in our faces, and was as dark as the fogs upon the banks of Newfoundland. Our strength and our hopes sunk together, nay, even those of reaching Carillon were doudtful, but we must proceed or perish. As it cleared up a little, we laboured to see the fort, which at every turn we expected, until we came to where the ice was gone, and the water narrow. This did not agree with my idea of South Bay, but it was no time for reflection; we quitted the ice to the left, and after marching two miles, our guide assured us we ought to be on the other side of the water. This was a very distressing circumstance, yet we returned to the ice and passed to the right, where, after struggling through the snow, about four miles, and breaking in every second step, as we had no snow-shoes, we were stopped by a large water-fall. Here I was again astonished with appearances, but nothing now was to be thought of only reaching the fort before night; yet to pass this place seemed impracticable: however, I attempted to ford it a little higher, and had almost gained the opposite shore, where the depth of the water, which was up to my breast, and the rapidity of the stream, hurried me off the slippery rocks, and plunged me entirely in the waters. I was obliged to quit my fuzee, and with great difficulty escaped being carried down the fall. Mr. ———, who followed me, and the guide, though they held by one another, suffered the same fate; but the hopes of soon reaching a fire made us think lightly of this: as night approached, we laboured excessively through the snow; we were certain the fort was not far from us, but our guide confessed, for the first time, that he was at a loss. Here we plainly observed that his brain was affected: he saw Indians all around him, and though we have since learned we had every thing to fear from them, yet it was

83

a danger we did not now attend to; nay, we shouted aloud several times to give information we were there; but we could neither hear nor see any body to lead us right, or more likely to destroy us, and if we halted a minute we became pillars of ice; so that we resolved, as it froze so hard, to make a fire, although the danger was apparent. Accidentally we had one dry cartridge, and in trying with my pistol if it would flash a little of the powder, Mr.———unfortunately held the cartridge too near, by which it took fire, blew up in our faces, almost blinded him, and gave excessive pain. This indeed promised to be the last stroke of fortune, as our hopes of a fire were now no more; but although we were not anxious about life, we knew it was more becoming to oppose than yield to this last misfortune. We made a path round a tree, and there exercised all the night, though scarcely able to stand, or prevent each other from sleeping. Our guide, notwithstanding repeated cautions, straggled from us, where he sat down and died immediately. On the morning of the 20th, we saw the fort, which we approached with a white flag: the officers run violently towards us, and saved us from a danger we did not then apprehend; for we are informed, that if the Indians, who were close after them, had seized us first, it would not have been in the power of the French to have prevented our being hurried to their camp, and perhaps to Montreal the next day, or killed for not being able to march. Mons. Debecourt and all his officers treat us with humanity and politeness, and are solicitous in our recovery, which returns slowly, as you may imagine, from all these difficulties; and though I have omitted many, yet I am afraid you will think me too prolix; but we wish, Sir, to persuade you of a truth, that nothing but the situation I have faithfully described could determine us in a resolution which appeared only one degree preferable to perishing in the woods.

I shall make no comments upon these distresses;

the malicious perhaps will say, which is very true, we brought them upon ourselves; but let them not wantonly add, we deserved them because we were unsuccessful. They must allow we could not be led abroad, at such a season of snow and ice, for amusement, or by an idle curiosity. I gave you, Sir, my reasons for asking leave, which you were pleased to approve, and I hope will defend them; and the same would make me again, as a volunteer, experience the chance of war to-morrow, had I an opportunity. These are Mr. ———'s sentiments as well as mine; and we both know you, Sir, too well, to harbour the least doubt of receiving justice with regard to our conduct in this affair, or our promotion in the regiment; the prospect of not joining that so soon as we flattered ourselves has depressed our spirits to the lowest degree, so that we earnestly beg you will be solicitous with the General to have us restored as soon as possible, or at least to prevent our being sent to France, and separated from you, perhaps, during the war.

I have but one thing more to add, which we learned here, and which perhaps you have already observed from what I have said, that we were upon no other ice than that of Lake George; but by the day overtaking us, the morning of the 14th, in the very place we had, in coming, marched during the night, we were entirely unacquainted with it, and obliged to put confidence in this guide, whose head must have been astray from the beginning, or he could not so grossly have mistaken a place where he had so often been. This information but added to our distress, until we reflected that our not being entirely lost was the more wonderful. That we had parted from South Bay on the 14th, was a point with us beyond all doubt, and about which we never once hesitated, so that we acted entirely contrary to what we had established as a truth; for if, according to that, we had continued our course to the west, we must inevitably have perished; but the hand of Providence led us back contrary to our judgement; and though even then, and often afterwards, we thought it severe, yet in the end it saved us, and obliged us to rest satisfied that we construed many things unfortunate, which tended to our preservation.

I am, &c.

Upon my return from the late unfortunate scout, I was ordered to Albany to recruit my companies, where I met with a very friendly reception from my Lord How, who advanced me cash to recruit the Rangers, and gave me leave to wait upon General Abercrombie at New York, who had now succeeded my Lord Loudoun in the chief command, my Lord being at this time about to embark for England. I here received a commission from the General, of which the following is a copy.

By his Excellency James Abercromby, Esq; Colonel of His Majesty's 44th Regiment of Foot, Colonel in Chief of the 60th or Royal American Regiment, Major General and Commander in Chief of all his Majesty's Forces raised or to be raised in North America, &c. Whereas it may be of great use to his Majesty's service in the operations now carrying on for recovering his rights in America, to have a number of men employed in obtaining intelligence of the strength, situation, and motions of the enemy, as well as other services, for which Rangers, or men acquainted with the woods, only are fit: Having the greatest confidence in your loyalty, courage and skill in this kind of service, I do, by virtue of the power and authority to me given by his Majesty, hereby constitute and appoint you to be Major of the Rangers in his Majesty's service, and likewise Captain of a company of said Rangers. You are therefore to take the said Rangers as Major, and the said Company as Captain, into your care and charge, and duly exercise and instruct, as well the officers as the soldiers thereof, in arms, and to use your best endeavours to keep them in good order and discipline; and I do hereby command them to obey you as their Major and Captain respectively, and you are to follow and observe such orders and directions from time to time as you shall receive from his Majesty, myself, or any other superior officer, according to the rules and discipline of war.

Given at New York, this 6th day of April 1758, in the thirty-first Year of the reign of our Sovereign Lord George the second, by the Grace of God, King of Great Britain, France and Ireland, Defender of the Faith, &c.

JAMES ABERCROMBY.

By his Excellency's command,

J. APPY.

I left New York April 18, and according to orders attended Lord How at Albany, for his directions, on the 12th, with whom I had a most agreeable interview, and a long conversation concerning the methods of distressing the enemy, and prosecuting the war with vigour the ensuing campaign. I parted with him, having the strongest assurances of his friendship and influence in my behalf, to wait upon Colonel Grant, commanding officer at Fort Edward, to assist in conducting the Rangers, and scouting parties, in such amanner as might best serve the common cause, having a letter from my Lord to him.

Capt. Stark was immediately dispatched to Ticonderoga on the west-side of Lake George. Capt. Jacob, whose Indian name was Nawnawapeteoonks, on the east-side, and Capt Shepherd betwixt the lakes, with directions to take if possible some prisoners near Carillon.

About the same time I marched myself with eighteen men for Crown Point. Capt. Burbank was likewise dispatched in quest of prisoners. These scouts, being often relieved, were kept out pretty constantly, in order to discover any parties of the enemy that might sally out towards our forts or frontiers, and to reconnoitre their situation and motions from time to time. The success of my scout was as follows.

April 29, 1758

I marched from Fort Edward with a party of eighteen men, up the road that leads to Fort William Henry four miles, then north four miles, and encamped at Schoon Creek, it having been a very rainy day.

On the 30th we marched north-and-by-east all day, and encamped near South-Bay.

The 1st of May we continued the same course, and at night encamped near the narrows, north of South Bay.

The 2d, in the morning, made a raft, and crossed the bay over to the east-side, and having distanced the lake about four miles we encamped.

The 3d we steered our course north, and lay at night about three miles from Carillon.

The 4th we marched north-by-east all day, and encamped at night three miles from Crown Point Fort.

The 5th we killed one Frenchman, and took three prisoners.

The 6th, in the morning, began our return homeward, and arrived with our prisoners at Fort Edward the 9th.

One of the prisoners, who appeared to be the most intelligible, reported, "that he was born in Lorrain in France; that he had been in Canada eight years, viz two at Quebec, one at Montreal, and five at Crown Point; that at the latter were about 200 soldiers, of which Mons. le Janong was commander in chief; that at Ticonderoga there were 400 of the Queen's regiment, 150 marines, 200 Canadians, and about 700 Indians; and that they daily expected 300 Indians more; that they did not intend to attack our forts this summer, but were preparing to receive us at Ticonderoga; that they had heard that I, with most of my party, was killed in the conflict last March; but afterwards, by some prisoners which a small party of their Indians had taken from Dutch Hoosyk, they were informed that Rogers was yet alive, and was going to attack them again, being fully resolved to revenge the inhumanity and barbarity with which they had used his men, in particular Lieut. Philips and his party, who were butchered by them, after they had promised them quarters; that this was talked of among the Indians, who greatly blamed the French for encouraging them so to do."

Captains Stark and Jacob returned the day before me; the former brought in with him six prisoners, four of which he took near Ticonderoga; they having escaped from New York and Albany, were in their flight to the French forts. The latter, who had but one white man with him, and eighteen Indians, took ten prisoners, and seven scalps, out of a party of fifty French. An account of these scouts, and the intelligence thereby gained, was transmitted to my Lord How, and by him to the General.

About the middle of May, a flag of truce was sent to Ticonderoga, on Col. Schyler's account, which put a stop to all offensive scouts, till its return.

May 28, 1758

I received positive orders from the General, to order all officers and men, belonging to the Rangers, and the two Indian companies, who were now on furlow, or recruiting parties, to join their respective companies as soon as possible, and that every man of the corps under my command should be at his post at or before the 10th of the month. These orders were obeyed, and parties kept out on various scouts till the 8th of June, when my Lord How arrived at Fort Edward with one half of the army.

His Lordship immediately ordered me out with fifty men in whale-boats, which were carried over in waggons to Lake George, and directed me at all events to take a plan of the landing-place at the north-end with all possible accuracy, and also of the ground from the landing-place to the French fort at Carillon, and of Lake Champlain for three miles beyond it, and to discover the enemy's number in that quarter. Agreeable to these orders, on the 12th in the morning, I marched with a party of fifty men, and encamped in the evening at the place where Fort William-Henry stood.

On the 30th we proceeded down the lake in five whale-boats to the first narrows, and so on to the west-end of the lake, where I took the plan his Lordship desired. Part of my party then proceeded to reconnoitre Ticonderoga, and discovered a large encampment there, and a great number of Indians. While I was, with two or three others, taking a plan of the fort, encampment, &c. I left the remainder of my party at some considerable distance; when I was returning to them, at the distance of about 300 yards, they were fallen upon by a superior number of the enemy who had got between me and them. Capt. Jacobs, with the Mohegon Indians, run off at the first onset, calling to our people to run likewise; but they stood their ground, and discharged their pieces several times at last broke through the enemy, by whom they were surrounded on all sides except their rear, where a river covered them: they killed three of the enemy, but lost eight of their own party in this skirmish. My party rallied at the boats, where I joined them and having collected all but the slain together, we returned homewards. On the 20th, at Half Way brook, we met Lord How, advanced with three thousand men, to whom I gave an account of my scout, together with a plan of the landing-place, the fort at Carillon, and the situation of the lakes.

I obtained leave from my Lord to go to Fort Edward, where his excellency Major General Abercrombie was then posted, who ordered me to join my Lord How the next day with all the Rangers, being 600, in order to proceed with his Lordship to the Lake.

On the 22nd his Lordship encamped at the lake where formerly stood Fort William-Henry, and ordered the Rangers to advance 400 yards on the west-side, and encamp there; from which place, by his Lordship's orders, I sent off next morning three small parties of Rangers, viz. one to the narrows of South Bay, another to the west-side of Lake George, and a third to Ticonderoga Fort, all three parties by land. Another party, consisting of two Lieutenants and seventeen men, proceeded down the lake for discoveries, and were all made prisoners by about 300 French and Indians. This party embarked in whale-boats.

About the 28th of June his Excellency Major General Abercrombie arrived at the lake with the remainder of the army, where he tarried till the morning of the 5th of July, and then the whole army, consisting of near 16,000, embarked in battoes for Ticonderoga.

The order of march was a most agreeable sight; regular troops in the center, provincials on each wing, the light infantry on the right of the advanced guard, the Rangers on the left, with Colonel Broadstreet's battoes in the center. In this manner we proceeded, till dusk, down Lake George, to Sabbath Day Point, where the army halted and refreshed. About ten o'clock the army moved again, when my Lord How went in the front with his whale-boat, Lieutenant Col. Broadstreet's and mine, with Lieutenant Holmes, in another, whom he sent forward to go near the landing place, and observe if any enemy was posted there.

Holmes returned about day-break, met the army near the Blue Mountains within four miles of the landing-place, and reported that there was a party of the enemy at the landing-place, which he discovered by their fires.

As soon as it was light his Lordship, with Col. Broadstreet and myself, went down to observe the landing-place before the army, and when within a quarter of a mile, plainly discerned that it was but a small detachment of the enemy that was there; whereupon his Lordship said he would return to the General, that the army might land and march to Ticonderoga.

About twelve o'clock the whole army landed, the Rangers on the left wing. I immediately sent an officer to wait upon the General for his orders, and received directions from Capt. Abercrombie, one of his Aids de Camp, to gain the top of a mountain that bore north about a mile from the landing-place, and from thence steer east to the river that runs into the falls betwixt the landing and the saw-mill, to take possession of some rising ground on the enemy's side, and there to wait the army's coming.

I immediately marched, ascended the top of the hill, and from thence marched to the place I was ordered, where I arrived in about an hour, and posted my party to as good advantage as I could, being within one quarter of a mile of where Mons. Montcalm was posted with 1500 men, whom I had discovered by some small reconnoitring parties sent out for that purpose.

About twelve o'clock Colonels Lyman and —tch of the Provincials came to my rear, whom I informed of the enemy's being so very near, and inquiring concerning the army, they told me they were coming along. While this conversation passed, a sharp fire began in the rear of Col. Lyman's regiment, on which he said he would make his front immediately, and desired me to fall on their left flank, which I accordingly did, having first ordered Capt. Burbanks with 150 men to remain at the place where I was posted, to observe the motions of the French at the saw-mills, and went with the remainder of the Rangers on the left flank of the enemy, the river being on their right, and killed several.

By this time Lord Howe, with a detachment from his front, had broke the enemy, and hemmed them in on every side; but advancing himself with great eagerness and intrepidity upon them, was unfortunately shot and died immediately*.

There were taken prisoners of the enemy in this action, five officers, two volunteers, and one hundred and sixty men, who were sent to the landing place. Nothing more material was done this day.

The next morning, at six o'clock, I was ordered to march to the river that runs into the falls, the place where I was the day before, and there to halt on the west-side till further orders, with four hundred Rangers, while Captain Stark, with the remainder of the Rangers, marched with Capt. Abercrombie and Mr. Clerk the Engineer to observe the position of the enemy at the fort, from whence they returned again that evening.

The whole army lay the ensuing night under arms. By sunrise next morning, Sir William Johnson joined the army with four hundred and forty Indians. At seven o'clock I received orders to march with my Rangers. A Lieutenant of Captain Stark's led the advance guard. I was within

*This noble and brave officer being universally beloved by both officers and soldiers of the army, his fall was not only most sincerely lamented, but seemed to produce an almost general consternation and languor through the whole.

94

about three hundred yards of the breast-work when my advance guard was ambushed and fired upon by about 200 Frenchmen. I immediately formed a front, and marched up to the advanced guard, who maintained their ground, and the enemy immediately retreated; soon after the battoe-men formed on my left and light infantry on my right. This fire of the enemy did not kill a single man.

Soon after three regiments of Provincials came up and formed in my rear, at two hundred yards distance. While the army was thus forming, a scattering fire was kept up between our flying parties and those of the enemy without the breast-work. About half an hour past ten, the greatest part of the army being drawn up, a smart fire began on the left wing, where Col. De Lancey's, (the New Yorkers,) and the battoe-men were posted, upon which I was ordered forward to endeavour to beat the enemy within the breast-work, and then to fall down, that the pickets and grenadiers might march through.

The enemy soon retired within their works; Major Proby marched through with his pickets within a few yards of the breast-work, where he unhappily fell, and the enemy keeping up a heavy fire, the soldiers hastened to the right about, when Col. Haldiman came up with the grenadiers to support them, being followed by the battalions in brigades for their support. Col. Haldiman advanced very near the breast work, which was at least eight feet high; some of the provincials with the Mohocks came up also*.

We toiled with repeated attacks for four hours, being greatly embarrassed by trees that were felled by the enemy without their breast-work, when the General thought proper to order a retreat, directing me to bring up the rear, which I did in the dusk of the evening.

On the ninth in the evening, we arrived at our encampment

*This attack was begun before the General intended it should be, and as it were by accident, from the fire of the New Yorkers in the left wing; upon which Col. Haviland being in or near the center, ordered the troops to advance.

at the south-end of Lake George, where the army received the thanks of the General for their good behaviour, and were ordered to entrench themselves; the wounded were sent to Fort Edward and Albany.

Our loss both in the regular and provincial troops, was somewhat considerable. The enemy's loss was about five hundred, besides those who were taken prisoners.

July 8, 1758

By order of the General, I this day began a scout to South Bay, from which I returned the 16th, having effected nothing considerable, except discovering a large party of the enemy, supposed to be near a thousand, on the east-side of the lake. This party the next day, viz. the 17th, fell upon a detachment of Col. Nicholls's Regiment at the half-way brook, killed three Captains, and upwards of twenty private men.

The 27th another party of the enemy fell upon a convoy of waggoners between Fort Edward and Half-Way Brook, and killed 116 men, sixteen of which were Rangers. In persuit of this party, with a design to intercept their retreat, I was ordered to embark the 18th with 700 men; the enemy however escaped me, and in my return home on the 31st, I was met by an express from the General, with orders to march with 700 men to South and East Bay, and return by way of Fort Edward, in the prosecution of which orders nothing very material happened till the 8th of August; in our return, early in the morning of which day, we decamped from the place where Fort Anne stood, and began our march, Major Putnam with a party of Provincials marching in the front, my Rangers in the rear, Capt. Dalyell with the regulars in the center, the other officers suitably disposed among the men, being in number 530, exclusive of officers (a number having by leave returned home the day before.) After marching about three-quarters of a mile, a fire begun with five hundred of the enemy in the front; I brought my people into as good order as possible, Capt. Dalyell in the center, and the Rangers on the right, with Col. Partridge's light infantry; on the left was Capt. Gidding's of the Boston troops with his people, and Major

Putnam being in the front of his men when the fire began, the enemy rushing in, took him, one Lieutenant, and two others, prisoners, and considerably disordered others of the party, who afterwards rallied and did good service, particularly Lieutenant Durkee, who notwithstanding two wounds, one in his thigh, the other in his wrist, kept in the action the whole time, encouraging his men with great earnestness and resolution.

Capt. Dalyell with Gage's light infantry, and Lieut. Eyers of the 44th regiment, behaved with great bravery, they being in the center, where was at first the hottest fire, which afterwards fell to the right where the Rangers were, and where the enemy made four different attacks; in short, officers and soldiers throughout the detachment behaved with such vigour and resolution, as in one hour's time broke the enemy, and obliged them to retreat, which they did with such caution in small scattering parties, as gave us no great opportunity to distress them by a pursuit; we kept the field and buried our dead.

When the action was over, we had missing fifty-four men, twenty-one of which afterwards came in, being separated from us while the action continued. The enemy's loss was 199 killed on the spot, several of which were Indians*.

We arrived at Fort Edward on the 9th, being met at some distance from it by Col. Provost, with a party of 300, and refreshments for the wounded, which I had desired by an express sent before.

I remained at Fort Edward till the 11th of the month, when I received orders from Col. Provost, who now ranked as Brigadier, and commanded at Fort Edward, to march and pursue the tracks of a large party of Indians, of which he had received intelligence, down the east-side of Hudson's River, in order to secure our convoys from them, and intercept their retreat; but this report which the Colonel had heard being

*By a detachment that went out afterwards, fifty more of the enemy were found dead near the place of action.

groundless, my scout was ineffectual. I returned to Fort Edward on the 14th, and went with my detachment directly to the encampment at Lake George.

August 20, 1758

By orders from the General I embarked with five men in a whale-boat, to visit and reconnoitre Ticonderoga, in which excursion I obtained several articles of intelligence concerning the enemy, their situation and numbers at different posts, and returned the 24th to the encampment at Lake George.

I was employed in various other excursions towards rhe enemy's forts and frontiers, and in persuit of their flying parties, till the campaign for this year ended, and our army retired to winter-quarters.

Notwithstanding little was effected by our late campaign to Ticonderoga; yet the British arms in America were not every where unsuccessful: for Col. Broadstreet, with a detachment of 2000 men, reduced the French fort at Cataraqua, called Fort Frontenac⋆, and General Amherst, who commanded the British troops at Cape Breton, had succeeded in the reduction of that important fortress, and now returned from his conquest, with a part of the troops that had been employed there, and was appointed commander in chief of his Majesty's forces in North America (General Abercrombie embarking for England). The head quarters were now fixed at New York, and I had now new commanders to obey, new companions to converse with, and, as it were, a new apprenticeship to serve. From Albany, where I was settling some accounts with the Paymaster, I began my acquaintance by the following letter to Col. Townsend, Deputy Adjutant General to his Excellency.

⋆*This fort was square faced, had four bastions built with stone, and was near three-quarters of a mile in cicumference. Its situation was very beautiful, the banks of the river presenting on every side an agreeable landscape, with a fine prospect of Lake Ontario, which was distant about a league, interspersed with many islands that were well wooded, and seemingly fruitful. The French had formerly a great trade at this fort with the Indians, it being erected on purpose to prevent their trading with the English; but it is now totally destroyed.*

Sir,

Inclosed I send you the present state of his Majesty's companies of Rangers at Fort Edward, together with a list of the officers, now recruiting in the different parts of New England, who have lately advised me, that they have already inlisted near 400 men, which recruits are much wanted at Fort Edward, as it may be expected that the enemy will soon send their Indians, to endeavour to intercept our convoys between here and Fort Edward.

To be seasonably strong to prevent their playing their old pranks, I would humbly propose, were it consistent with the service and agreeable to General Amherst, my setting out for New England, in order to dispatch such Rangers as there are with all possible speed to Fort Edward, or otherwise, as his Excellency shall direct. If it should be agreeable to the General that I should go to New England, I should be glad it might be by way of New York, that I might have an opportunity to wait upon the General myself, and represent to him the necessity of an augmentation of the Rangers now at Fort Edward, and the desire of the Stockbridge Indians to re-enter the service.

The arms of the Rangers are in the hands of Mr. Cunningham at New York, which will soon be wanted at Fort Edward, I should therefore be glad they might be forwarded as soon as may be. I have wrote to Mr. Cunningham, to make application to you for convenient carriages for the same, which I should be glad you would furnish him with. And till the time I have an opportunity of paying you my respects in person, I beg leave to subscribe myself, Sir,

Your most obedient humble servant,

Robert Rogers.

P.S. General Stanwix informs me, that a subaltern officer, and about twenty Rangers, are to be stationed at No.4; the officer I would recommend for that post, is Lieut. Stephans, who is well acquainted with the country there-about. He is now recruiting.

To Col. Townsend.

Soon after this I returned to Fort Edward, where I received the Colonel's answer, as follows.

Feb. 5, 1759

Sir,

I received your letter, with the inclosed return. The General commands me to inform you, he can by no means approve of your leaving Fort Edward.

Your recruiting officers are all ordered to send up their recruits to Fort Edward. They are not only wrote to, but an advertisement is put in all the papers, which was the only method the General had of conveying his intentions to them, as you had not sent me any return of the officers names, and places where they were to recruit at. In obedience to that order, the recruits will be up sooner than if they waited your coming down. I have likewise repeated the order to every officer, according to your return, by this post, and if you are complete by the returns they make, I shall order up every individual officer to their posts.

Any proposals for the augmentation of the Rangers, or proposals from the Stockbridge Indians, you would chuse to offer to the General, he desires may be immediately sent down to him.

The arms for the Rangers, which you mention are in the hands of Mr. Cunningham, shall be sent up to you immediately.

I have wrote to Lieut. Samuel Stephans, to acquaint him with the General's intentions of leaving him at No.4.

If the enemy send out any scouting parties this year to pick up intelligence, or attack our convoys, the season of the year is now coming on that we may expect them; you therefore must see the necessity of your remaining at Fort Edward. Your officers and men should join you as fast as possible. The General would at another time comply with your request.

Your obedient humble servant,

R. *Townshend,* D. A.G.

To Major Rogers.   *Feb.* 15, 1759.

I wrote to the colonel, proposing an addition of two new companies of Rangers, upon the same footing as those already in the service, and the raising of three companies of Indians to serve the ensuing campaign; and lest the Indians should be gone out on their hunting parties, and so be prevented from joining us, I wrote to three of their Sachems, or chiefs; one of which to King Uncus, head Sachem of the Mohegan Indians (which in substance is like the others) I will here insert, as a specimen of the method in which we are obliged to address these savages.

Brother Uncus,

As it is for the advantage of his Majesty King George, to have a large body of Rangers employed in his service the ensuing campaign, and as I am well convinced of the sincere attachment you have to him, I therefore carefully obey General Amherst's orders to me, to engage your assistance here early in the spring.

I hope you will continue to shew that ardent zeal you have all along expressed for the English, ever since you have been allied to them, by raising a company of your men with the utmost expedition.

Should you chuse to come out a Captain, General Amherst will readily give you the commission for it; if not, I shall expect Doquipe and Nunnipad. I leave to you the choice of an Ensign and two serjeants; but I hope you'll engage the fittest men for their stations. I would have the company consist of fifty private men, or more, if you can get them; and if those men that deserted from Capt. Brewer will join you, the General will pardon them. You may employ a Clerk for the company, to whom General Amherst will allow the usual pay.

I heartily wish you success in raising your men and shall be exceeding glad that you join me with all the expedition you possibly can. I am,

Brother Uncus,

Your most obedient humble servant,

Robert Rogers.

To King Uncus.

With this letter, or any other wrote to them, in order to give it any credit or influence, must go a belt of wampum, suitable to the matter and occasion of it, and upon which the bearer, after having read the letter, interprets it, and then delivers both to the Sachem, or person they are directed to.

The latter end of February, about fifty Mohocks, commanded by Captain Lotridge, came from Sir William Johnson to join me, and proceed to Ticonderoga on a scout.

March 3, 1759

I received the following orders from Col. Haldiman:

An officer being chosen by the General to make observations upon the enemy's situation, and the strength of their forts upon Lake Champlain, you are ordered to march with your Rangers, and the Mohock Indians, under the command of Capt. Lotridge, and take all the measures and precautions possible, that he may execute his intentions, and perform the service, which the General has much at heart; and to effect this with more security, a body of regulars is likewise ordered to join with you, and you are to have the command of the whole. Lieut. Brheem is to communicate his orders to you; and the service being performed, you will endeavour to take a prisoner, or prisoners, or strike such a stroke on the enemy, and try to bring us intelligence.

He recommends it in the strongest manner, that if some of the enemy should fall into your hands, to prevent the Indians from exercising their cruelty upon them, as he desires prisoners may be treated with humanity.

Fred. Haldiman,
Commander at
Fort Edward.

Fort Edward,
March 3, 1759.

Pursuant to the above orders, I marched the same day with a party of 358 men, officers included, and encamped the first night at Half-Way Brook. One Indian, being hurt by accident, returned to Fort Edward.

The 4th, marched to within one mile and a half of Lake George, and halted till evening, that we might the better pass undiscovered by the enemy, if any were on the hill reconnoitering. We continued to march till two o'clock in the morning, and halted at the first narrows. It being excessive cold, and several of our party being frost-bitten, I sent back twenty-three, under the charge of a careful serjeant, to Fort Edward. We continued here till the evening of the 5th, then Marched to Sabbath-day Point, where we arrived about eleven o'clock, almost overcome with cold. At two o'clock we continued our march, and reached the landing-place about eight. I sent out a small party to observe if any of the enemy's parties went out. They returned and reported, that none were to be seen on the west-side of the lake, but on the east were two working parties.

It now appeared to be a suitable time for the Engineer to make his observations. I left Capt. Williams to remain at this place with the Regulars, and thirty Rangers, while I, with the engineer, forty-nine Rangers, and Capt. Lotridge, with forty-five Indians, went to the isthmus that overlooks the fort, where he made his observations. We returned to our party, leaving five Indians and one Ranger to observe what numbers crossed the lake in the evening from the east-side to the fort, that I might know the better how to attack them next morning. At dark the engineer went again, with Lieut. Tute, and a guard of ten men, to the entrenchments, and returned at midnight without opposition, having done his business to his satisfaction.

On which I ordered Capt. Williams with the Regulars back to Sabbath-day Point; the party being extremely distressed with the cold, it appeared to me imprudent to march his men any further, especially as they had no snow-shoes. I sent with him Lieut. Tute and thirty Rangers, with directions to kindle fires on the aforesaid point.

At three o'clock I marched with three Lieutenants and forty Rangers, one Regular, and Capt. Lotridge with forty-six Indians, in order to be ready to attack the enemy's working parties on the east-side of the lake early in the morning. We crossed South-Bay about eight miles south of the fort*; from thence, it being about six o'clock, bore down right opposite the fort, and within half a mile of where the French parties, agreeable to our expectations, were cutting of wood. Here I halted, and sent two Indians and two Rangers to observe their situation. They returned in a few minutes, and brought intelligence, that the working parties were close to the banks of the lake, and opposite the fort, and were about forty in number; upon which we stripped off our blankets, and ran down upon them, took several prisoners, and destroyed most of the party as they were retreating to the fort, from whence being discovered, about eighty Canadians and Indians pursued us closely, being backed by about 150 French regulars, and in a mile's march they began a fire in our rear; and as we marched in a line abreast, our front was easily made; I halted on a rising ground, resolving to make a stand against the enemy, who appeared at first very resolute: but we repulsed them before their reinforcement came up, and began our march again in a line abreast; having advanced about half a mile further, they came in sight again.

As soon as we could obtain an advantageous post, which was a long ridge, we again made a stand on the side opposite the enemy. The Canadians and Indians came very close, but were soon stopped by a warm fire from the Rangers and Mohocks. They broke immediately, and the Mohocks with some rangers pursued, and entirely routed them before their Regulars could come up. After this we marched without any opposition. In these several skirmishes we had two Rangers and one Regular killed, and one Indian wounded, and killed about thirty of the enemy.

We coninued our march till twelve o'clock at night, and came to Capt. Williams at Sabbath-day Point (fifty miles distant from the place we set out from in the morning.) The Captain

*Here we found that a party of Indians had gone up the bay towards our forts.

received us with good fires, than which scarce anything could be more acceptable to my party, several of which had their feet froze, it being excessive cold, and the snow four feet deep.

Next morning marched the whole detachment as far as Long Island in Lake George, and there encamped that night. On our march from Sabbath-day Point to this island, I gave leave to some of the Rangers and Indians to hunt near the side of the lake, who brought us in great plenty of venison for our refreshment.

I sent Lieut. Tute, with the following letter, to Col. Haldiman, fearing lest a party of Indians we had some notice of might have gone up South Bay, and get an opportunity of doing mischief before I could reach Fort Edward with the whole detachment.

> *Camp at Sabbath-day Point, Friday*
> *eight o'clock in the morning.*
>
> Sir,
>
> I send this to let you know that sixty Indians, in two parties, are gone towards Fort Edward and Saratoga, and I fear will strike some blow before this reaches you. Mr. Brheem is satisfied that he has done his business agreeable to his orders; since which I have taken some prisoners from Ticonderoga, and destroyed others of the enemy, of the particulars of which the bearer will inform you.
>
> The Mohocks behaved with great bravery; some have been within pistol-shot of the French fort.
>
> Two-thirds of my detachment have froze their feet (the weather being so severe, that it is almost impossible to describe it) some of which we are obliged to carry. I am, &c.
>
> R. Rogers.
>
> *Fort Edward, March* 10, 1759.

Dear Sir,

I congratulate you heartily on your good success, and send you twenty-two sleys to transport your sick. You will, by this opportunity, take as many boards as you can conveniently★. My best compliments to Capt. Williams, and to all the gentlemen. I am, Sir,

Your most humble servant,

Fred. Haldimand,

P.S. I had the signal-guns fired to give notice to the different posts. Nothing has appeared as yet★★,

We were met by the sleys, and a detachment of 100 men at Lake George, and all arrived safe at Fort Edward, where I received the following letters upon my arrival.

SIR,

I yesterday received your letter by Mr. Stark. The General approves of raising the Indian companies; but as he has not heard the Rangers are complete, he cannot agree to the raising more companies, till the present ones are complete at Fort Edward. Mr. Stark sets out to-morrow for New England. I have ordered him to hurry up the recruits of your corps, and repeat my orders to the officers, to join their companies if they are complete. Your arms have been tried and proved by the artillery; they answer very well, and are ordered to be sent to you as fast as possible: the General has sent to you by Capt. Jacobs. We have chose out one hundred men from each regiment, and pitched upon the officers to act this year as light infantry; they are cloathed and accoutred as light as possible, and, in my opinion, are a kind of troops that

★*Boards left at the place where Fort William-Henry stood, and now wanted for Fort Edward.*
★★*The explosion of these signal-guns (as we afterwards heard) was heard by the party of the enemy, then near Fort Millar, eight miles below Fort Edward, who thereupon supposing themselves discovered, retreated with precipitation.*

has been much wanted in this country. They have what ammunition they want, so that I don't doubt but they will be excellent marksmen. You may depend upon General Amherst's intentions to have you; I heard Brigadier Gage mention you to him. From what knowledge I have of the General, I can only say that merit is sure to be rewarded; nor does he favour any recommendation, without the person recommended really deserves his promotion. You will return your companies to me as soon as complete.

Your obedient humble servant,

R. Townshend.

New York,
Feb. 26, 1759.
To Major Rogers.

New York, Feb. 13, 1759.

SIR,

This will be delivered to you by Capt. Jacob Nawnawampeteoonk, who last campaign commanded a company of Stockbridge Indians, and who, upon hearing that you had wrote to me concerning him, came to offer me his service for the ensuing campaign: But as you have not mentioned to me the terms and conditions on which he was to engage, I have referred him to you to give in his proposals, that you may report to me thereupon, and inform me if you think his servce adequate to them; after which I shall give you my answer. I am, Sir,

Your very humble servant,

Jeff. Amherst.

To Major Rogers.

Before I received this letter from his Excellency, I had wrote to him, recommending several officers to the vacancies in the ranging companies, and inclosed a journal of my late scout;

soon after my return from which I went to Albany, to settle my accompts with the government, where I waited upon his Excellency the General, by whom I was very kindly received, and assured that I should have the rank of Major in the army from the date of my commission under General Abercrombie.

I returned to Fort Edward the fifteenth of May, where I received the melancholy news, that Capt. Burbank, with a party of thirty men, had in my absence been sent out on a scout, and were all cut off. This gave me me great uneasiness, as Mr. Burbank was a gentleman I very highly esteemed, and one of the best officers among the Rangers, and more especially as I judged the scout he was sent out upon by the commanding officer at the fort was needless, and unadvisedly undertaken.

Preparations for the campaign were hastened by his Excellency the General in every quarter; the levies from the several provinces forwarded, the companies of Rangers compleated, and disciplined in the best manner I was capable of, and of which the General was pleased greatly to approve.

In the month of June, part of the army marched with General Gage for the lake. I was ordered to send three companies there with Capt. Stark, and to remain with the General myself with the other three companies, till such time as he marched thither. In this interval, pursuant to his Excellency's orders, I sent out several parties to the French forts, who from time to time discovered the situation of the enemy, and brought satisfactory intelligence.

About the 20th of June, the General with the remainder of the army marched to the lake, the Rangers being in the advanced guard; and here his Excellency was pleased to fulfil his promise to me, by declaring in public orders, my rank of Major in the army, from the date of my commission, as Major of the Rangers. We continued here collecting our strength together, and making necessary preparations, and getting what intelligence we could of the strength and situation of the enemy, till July 21, 1759, when the army embarked for

Ticonderoga. I was in the front with the Rangers on the right wing, and was the first body that landed on July 22, at the north-end of Lake George, followed by the grenadiers and light infantry, which Col. Haviland commanded.

I marched, agreeable to orders from the General, across the mountains in the isthmus; from thence, in a by-way, athwart the woods to the bridge at the Saw-mills; where finding the bridge standing, I immediately crossed it with my Rangers, and took possession of the rising ground on the other side, and beat from thence a party of the enemy, and took several prisoners, killed others, and put the remainder to flight, before Col. Haviland with his grenadiers and light infantry got over. The army took possession that night of the heights near the Saw-mills, where they lay all this evening.

The enemy kept out a scouting-party, with a body of Canadians and Indians, which killed several of our men, and galled us prodigiously.

July 23, 1759

The General, early in the morning, put the army in motion; at the same time ordered me in the front, with directions to proceed across the Chesnut Plain, the nighest and best way I could, to Lake Champlain, and do my endeavour to strike it near the edge of the cleared ground, between that and the breastwork, where I was to halt till I received further orders. Having pursued my orders, and halted at the lake, I informed the General of my situation, and that nothing extaordinary had happened in our march.

The General by this time had appointed and formed a detachment to attack their main breast-work on the hill, and had got possession of it. I was ordered to send two hundred men to take possession of a small entrenchment next to Lake Champlain; and Captain Brewer, whom I had sent to take possession of this post, happily succeeded.

From the time the army came in sight the enemy kept up a constant fire of cannon from their walls and batteries at our people.

The General at this time had left several Provincial regiments to bring the cannon and ammunition across the Carrying Place, together with provisions, which they did with great expedition*.

---

*About this time some of the Provincial regiments were sent to Oswego, to assist in building a fort there.

July 24, 1759

All this day the engineers were employed in raising batteries, as was likewise a great part of the army in that work, and in making and fetching fascines, till the 26th at night; all which time I had parties out to Crown Point to watch the motions of the enemy there; by which means the General had not only daily, but hourly intelligence from those posts.

I this day received orders from the General to attempt to cut away a boom which the French had thrown across the lake opposite the fort, which prevented our boats from passing by, and cutting off their retreat. For the completion of this order I had sixty Rangers in one English flat-bottomed boat and two whale-boats*, in which, after night came on, I embarked, and passed over to the other side of Lake Champlain, opposite to the Rangers encampment, and from that intended to steer my course along the east-shore, and privately saw off their boom, for which end I had taken saws with me, the booms being made with logs of timber.

About nine o'clock, when I had got about half way from the place where I had embarked, the enemy, who had undermined their fort, sprung their mines, which blew up with a loud explosion, the enemy being all ready to embark on board their boats, and make a retreat. This gave me an opportunity to attack them with such success as to drive several of them ashore; so that next morning we took from the east-shore ten boats, with a considerable quantity of baggage, and upwards of fifty barrels of powder, and large quantities of ball. About ten o'clock I returned, and made my report to the General.

The 27th I was ordered with my party to the Saw-mills

*These boats were carried across the land from Lake George to Lake Champlain, on which day the brave and worthy Col. Townshend was killed by a cannon ball from the enemy, whose fall was much lamented by the General.

(to wait the flying parties of the enemy which were expected that way) where I lay till the 11th of August*, on which day I received the following orders from General Amherst:

Sir,

You are this night to send a Captain, with a proper proportion of subalterns, and two hundred men, to Crown Point, where the officer is to post himself in such a manner as not to be surprised, and to seize on the best ground for defending himself; and if he should be attacked by the enemy, he is not to retreat with his party, but keep his ground till he is reinforced from the army. I am, Sir,

Your most obedient,

Jeff. Amherst.

To Major Rogers.

Capt. Brewer went with a party, and the General followed the 12th with the whole army, and the same day arrived at Crown Point, where it was found that Capt. Brewer had executed his orders extremely well.

This evening I had orders for encamping, and the ground for each corps being laid out, my camp was fixed in the front of the army. Immediately after the General had got the disposition of his camp settled, he began to clear ground, and prepare a place for erecting a new fort, in which service great part of the army was employed. I had orders to send Capt. Stark, with two hundred Rangers, to cut a road to No. 4. which party was immediately sent.

During these transactions I sent out (by the General's approbation) several scouting parties against the enemy**, which brought in prisoners from St. John's Fort, and others penetrated into the back country, the better to learn the nature and situation of it.

About this time a party of my people discovered that the enemy's Fort at Crown Point was likewise blown up, and the enemy fled.

**Capt. Tute, and Lieutenant Fletcher, in two different scouting parties, were taken and carried to Canada.*

Thus were we employed till the 12th of September, when the General, exasperated at the treatment which Capt. Kennedy had met with, who had been sent with a party as a flag of truce to the St. Francis Indians, with proposals of peace to them, and was by them made a prisoner with his whole party; this ungenerous inhumane treatment determined the General to chastise these savages with some severity, and, in order to it, I received from him the following orders, viz.

*You are this night to set out with the detachment as ordered yesterday, viz. of 200 men, which you will take under your command, and proceed to Misisquey Bay, from whence you will march and attack the enemy's settlements on the south-side of the river St. Lawrence, in such a manner as you shall judge most effectual to disgrace the enemy, and for the success and honour of his Majesty's arms.

Remember the barbarities that have been committed by the enemy's Indian scoundrels on every occasion, where they had an opportunity of shewing their infamous cruelties on the King's subjects, which they have done without mercy. Take your revenge, but don't forget that tho' those villains have dastardly and promiscuously murdered the women and children of all ages, it is my orders that no women or children are killed or hurt.

When you have executed your intended service, you will return with your detachment to camp, or to join me wherever the army may be.

Your's, &c.

Camp at Crown Point,   Jeff. Amherst.
Sept. 13, 1759.
To Major Rogers.

*That this expedition might be carried on with the utmost secrecy after the plan of it was concerted the day before the march, it was put into public orders, that I was to march a different way, at the same time I had private instructions to proceed directly to St. Francis.

In pursuance of the above orders, I set out the same evening with a detachment; and as to the particulars of my proceedings, and the great difficulties we met with in effecting our design, the reader is referred to the letter I wrote to General Amherst upon my return, and the remarks following it.

Copy of my Letter to the General upon my return from St. Francis:

Sir,

The twenty-second day after my departure from Crown Point, I came in sight of the Indian town of St. Francis in the evening, which I discovered from a tree that I climbed, at about three miles distance. Here I halted my party, which now consisted of 142 men, officers included, being reduced to that number by the unhappy accident which befel Capt. Williams*, and several since tiring, whom I was obliged to send back. At eight o'clock this evening I left the detachment, and took with me Lieut. Turner and Ensign Avery, and went to reconnoitre the town, which I did to my satisfaction, and found the Indians in a high frolic or dance. I returned to my party at two o'clock, and at three marched it to within five hundred yards of the town, where I lightened the men of their packs, and formed them for the attack.

At half an hour before sun-rise I surprised the town when they were all fast asleep, on the right, left, and center, which was done with so much alacrity by both the officers and men, that the enemy had not time to recover themselves, or take arms for their own defence, till they were chiefly destroyed, except some few of them who took to the water. About forty of my people pursued them, who destroyed such as attempted to make

---

*Capt. Williams of the Royal Regiment was, the fifth day of our march, accidentally burnt with gun-powder, and several men hurt, which, together with some sick, returned back to Crown Point, to the number of forty, under the care of Capt. Williams who returned with great reluctance.

their escape that way, and sunk both them and their boats. A little after sun-rise I set fire to all their houses, except three, in which there was corn, that I reserved for the use of the party.

The fire consumed many of the Indians who had concealed themselves in the cellars and lofts of their houses. About seven o'clock in the morning the affair was completely over, in which time we had killed at least two hundred Indians, and taken twenty of their women and children prisoners, fifteen of whom I let go on their own way, and five I brought with me, viz. two Indian boys, and three Indian girls. I likewise retook five English captives, which I also took under my care.

When I paraded my detachment, I found I had Capt. Ogden badly wounded in his body, but not so as to hinder him from doing his duty. I had also six men slightly wounded, and one Stockbridge Indian killed.

I ordered my people to take corn out of the reserved houses for their subsistence home, there being no other provision there; and whilst they were loading themselves I examined the prisoners and captives, who gave the following intelligence: "That a party of 300 French, and some Indians, were about four miles down the river below us; and that our boats were way-laid, which I had reason to believe was true, as they told the exact number, and the place where I left them at: that a party of 200 French and fifteen Indians had, three days before I attacked the town, gone up the river Wigwam Martinic, supposing that was the place I intended to attack;" whereupon I called the officers together, to consult the safety of our return, who were of opinion there was of no other way for us to return with safety, but by No. 4. on Connecticut River. I marched the detachment eight days in a body that way;

and when provisions grew scarce, near Ampara Magog Lake, I divided the detachment into small companies, putting proper guides to each, who were to assemble at the mouth of the Amonsook River*, as I expected provisions would be brought there for our relief**, not knowing which way I should return.

Two days after we parted, Ensign Avery, of Fitche's, fell in on my track, and followed in my rear; and a party of the enemy came upon them, and took seven of his party prisoners, two of whom that night made their escape, and came in to me next morning. Avery, with the remainder of his party, joined mine, and came with me to the Cohase Intervales, where I left them with Lieut. Grant, from which place I, with Capt. Ogden, and one man more, put down the river on a small raft to this place, where I arrived yesterday; and in half an hour after my arrival dispatched provisions up the river to Lieut. Grant in a canoe, which I am pretty certain will reach him this night, and next morning sent two other canoes up the river for the relief of the other parties, loaded with provisions, to the mouth of the Amonsook River.

I shall set off to go up the river myself to-morrow, to seek and bring in as many of our men as I can find, and expect to be back in about eight days, when I shall, with all expedition, return to Crown Point. As to other particulars relative to this scout, which your Excellency may think proper to inquire after, I refer you to Capt. Ogden, who bears this, and has accompanied me all the time I have been out, behaving very well. I am, Sir, with the greatest respect,

*Amonsook River falls into Connecticut River about sixty miles above No. 4.
**An officer, upon some intelligence that I had when going out, was sent back to Crown Point from Misisquey Bay, to desire that provisions might be conveyed to this place, as I had reason to believe we should be deprived of our boats, and consequently be obliged to return this way.

Your Excellency's most obedient servant,

No.4.   R.Rogers.

To General Amherst.   *Nov.* 5,1759.

I cannot forbear here making some remarks on the difficulties and distresses which attended us, in effecting this enterprize upon St. Francis, which is situated within three miles of the river St. Lawrence, in the middle of Canada, about half way betweem Montreal and Quebec.

It hath already been mentioned, how our party was reduced by the accident which befell Capt. Williams, the fifth day after our departure, and still farther by numbers tiring and falling sick afterwards. It was extremely difficult while we kept the water (and which retarded our progress very much) to pass undiscovered by the enemy, who were then cruizing in great numbers upon the lake; and had prepared certain vessels, on purpose to decoy any party of ours, that might come that way, armed with all manner of machines and implements for their destruction; but we happily escaped their snares of this kind, and landed (as hath been mentioned) the tenth day at Misisquey Bay. Here, that I might with more certainty know whether my boats (with which I left provision sufficient to carry us back to Crown Point) were discovered by the enemy, I left two trusty Indians to lie at a distance in sight of the boats, and there to stay till I came back, except the enemy found them; in which latter case they were with all possible speed to follow on my track, and give me intelligence.

It happened the second day after I left them, that these two Indians came up to me in the evening, and informed me that about 400 French had discovered and taken my boats, and that about one half of them were hotly pursuing on my track. This unlucky circumstance (it may well be supposed) put us into some consternation. Should the enemy overtake us, and we get the better of them in an encounter; yet being so far advanced into their country, where no reinforcement could possibly relieve us, and where they could be supported by any numbers they pleased, afforded us little hopes of escaping their hands.

Our boats being taken, cut off all hopes of a retreat by them; besides, the loss of our provisions left with them, of which we knew we should have great need at any rate, in case we survived, was a melancholy consideration. It was, however, resolved to prosecute our design at all adventures, and, when we had accomplished it, to attempt a retreat (the only possible way we could think of) by way of No. 4.; and that we might not be destroyed by famine in our return, I dispatched Lieut. McMullen by land to Crown Point, to desire of the General to relieve me with provision at Amonsook River, at the end of Cohase Intervales on Connecticut River, that being the way I should return, if at all, and the place appointed being about sixty miles from No. 4., then the most northerly English settlement. This being done, we determined if possible to outmarch our pursuers, and effect our design upon St. Francis before they could overtake us.

We marched nine days through wet sunken ground; the water most of the way near a foot deep, it being a spruce bog. When we encamped at night, we had no way to secure ourselves from the water, but by cutting the bows of trees, and with them erecting a kind of hammocks. We commonly began our march a little before day, and continued it till after dark at night.

The tenth day after leaving Misisquey Bay, we came to a river about fifteen miles above the town of St. Francis to the south of it; and the town being on the opposite or east side of it, we were obliged to ford it, which was attended with no small difficulty, the water being five feet deep, and the current swift. I put the tallest men up stream, and then holding by each other, we got over with the loss of several of our guns, some of which we recovered by diving to the bottom for them. We had now good dry ground to march upon, and discovered and destroyed the town as before related, which in all probability would have been effected with the loss of no man but the Indian who was killed in the action, had not my boats been discovered, and our retreat that way cut off.

This nation of Indians was notoriously attached to the French, and had for near a century past harrassed the frontiers of New England, killing people of all ages and sexes in a most barbarous manner, at a time when they did not in the least suspect them; and to my own knowledge, in six years time, carried into captivity, and killed, on the before mentioned frontiers, 400 persons. We found in the town hanging on poles over their doors, &c. about 600 scalps, mostly English.

The circumstances of our return are chiefly related in the preceding letter; however, it is hardly possible to describe the grief and consternation of those of us who came to Cohase Intervales. Upon our arrival there (after so many days tedious march over steep rocky mountains, or thro' wet dirty swamps, with the terrible attendants of fatigue and hunger) to find that here was no relief for us, where we had encouraged ourselves that we should find it, and have our distresses alleviated; for notwithstanding the officer I dispatched to the General discharged his trust with great expedition, and in nine days arrived at Crown Point, which was an hundred miles thro' the woods, and the General, without delay, sent Lieut. Stephans to No. 4. with orders to take provisions up the river to the place I had appointed, and there wait as long as there was any hopes of my returning; yet the officer that was sent being an indolent fellow, tarried at the place but two days, when he returned, taking all the provisions back with him, about two hours before our arrival. Finding a fresh fire burning in his camp, I fired guns to bring him back, which guns he heard, but would not return, supposing we were an enemy★.

Our distress upon this occasion was truly inexpressible; our

★*This gentleman, for this piece of conduct, was broke by a general court-martial, and rendered incapable of sustaining any office in his Majesty's service for the future: a poor reward, however, for the distresses and anguish thereby occasioned to so many brave men, to some of which it proved fatal, they actually dying with hunger.*

122

spirits, greatly depressed by the hunger and fatigues we had already suffered, now almost entirely sunk within us, seeing no resource left, nor any reasonable ground to hope that we should escape a most miserable death by famine.

At length I came to a resolution to push as fast as possible towards No. 4. leaving the remains of my party, now unable to march further, to get such wretched subsistence as the barren wilderness could afford*, till I could get relief to them, which I engaged to do within ten days.

I, with Capt. Ogden, one Ranger, and a captive Indian boy, embarked upon a raft we had made of dry pine-trees. The current carried us down the stream in the middle of the river, where we endeavoured to keep our wretched vessel by such paddles as we had made out of small trees, or spires split and hewed.

The second day we reached White River Falls, and very narrowly escaped being carried over them by the current. Our little remains of strength however enabled us to land, and to march by them. At the bottom of these falls, while Capt. Ogden and the Ranger hunted for red squirrels for refreshment, who had the good fortune likewise to kill a partridge, I attempted the forming a new raft for our further conveyance. Being not able to cut down trees, I burnt them down, and then burnt them off at proper lengths. This was our third day's work after leaving our companions.

The next day we got our materials together, and completed our raft, and floated with the stream again till we came to Wattockquitchey Falls, which are about fifty yards in length: here we landed, and by a wreath made of hazel bushes, Capt. Ogden held the raft, till I went to the bottom, prepared to swim in and board it when it came down, and if possible paddle it ashore, this being our only resource for life, as we were not able to make a third raft in case we had lost this. I had the good

*This was ground-nuts and lily roots, which being cleaned and boiled will serve to preserve life, and the use and method of preparing which I taught to Lieut. Grant, commander of the party.

fortune to succeed, and the next morning we embarked, and floated down the stream to within a small distance of No. 4. where we found some men cutting of timber, who gave us the first relief, and assisted us to the fort, from whence I dispatched a canoe with provisions, which reached the men at cohase four days after, which (agreeable to my engagement) was the tenth after I left them. Two days after my arrival at No. 4. I went with other canoes, loaded with provisions, up the river myself, for the relief of others of my party that might be coming in that way* having hired some of the inhabitants to assist me in this affair. I likewise sent expresses to Suncook and Pennecook upon Merrimack River, that any who should chance to straggle that way might be assisted; and provisions were sent up said rivers accordingly.

On my return to No. 4. I waited a few days to refresh such of my party as I had been able to collect together, and during my stay there received the following letter from General Amherst, in answer to mine of Nov. 5.

Crown Point, Nov. 8, 1759.

Sir,

Captain Ogden delivered me your letter of the 5th instant, for which I am not only to thank you, but to assure you of the satisfaction I had on reading it; as every step you inform me you have taken, has been very well judged, and deserves my full approbation. I am sorry Lieut. Stephans judged so ill in coming away with the provisions from the place where I sent him to wait for you.

An Indian is come in last night, and said he had left some of your party at Otter River. I sent for them; they are come in. This afternoon four Indians, two Rangers, a

---

* *I met several different parties; as Lieut. Curgill, Lieut. Campbell, Lieut. Farrington, and Serjeant Evans, with their respective divisions, and sent canoes further up for the relief of such as might be still behind, and coming this way. Some I met who escaped from Dunbar's and Turner's party, who were overtaken (being upwards of twenty innumber) and were mostly killed or taken by the enemy.*

German woman, and three other prisoners; they quitted four of your party some days since, and thought they had arrived here*. I am in hopes all the rest will get in very safe. I think there is no danger but they will, as you quitted them not till having marched eight days in a body; the only risk after that will be meeting hunting parties. I am, Sir,

Your humble servant,

To Major Rogers.   *Jeff. Amherst.*

As soon as my party were refreshed, such as were able I marched to Crown Point, where I arrived Dec.1, 1759, and upon examination found, that since our leaving the ruins of St. Francis, I had lost three officers, viz. Lieut. Dunbar of Gage's Light Infantry, Lieut. Turner of the Rangers, and Lieut. Jenkins of the Provincials, and forty-six serjeants and privates.

The Rangers at that place were all dismissed before my return, excepting two companies, commanded by Captains Johnson and Tute**, with whom I found orders left by the General for me to continue at that garrison during the winter, but had leave, however, to go down the country, and to wait upon his excellency at New York.

After giving in my return to the General, and what intelligence I could of the enemy's situation, he desired me, when I had leisure, to draw a plan of my march to St. Francis; and then, by his order, I returned by way of Albany; which place I left the 6th of February 1760, with thirteen recruits I had inlisted; and the 13th, on my way between Ticonderoga and Crown Point, my party was attacked by about sixty Indians, who killed five, and took four prisoners. I, with the remainder, made my escape to Crown Point, from whence I would have pursued them immediately; but Col. Haviland, the

* *Upon our separation, some of the divisions were ordered to make for Crown Point, that being the best route for hunting.*
** *Capt. Tute, who had been taken prisoner, was returned by a flag of truce, while I was gone to St. Francis.*

commanding officer there, judged it not prudent, by reason the garrison at that time was very sickly★. I continued at Crown Point the remainder of the winter.

On the 31st of March, Capt. James Tute, with two regular officers and six men, went out a scouting, and were all made prisoners; the enemy was not pursued, on account of the sickness of the garrison.

The same day I received from General Amherst the following letter.

New York, March 1, 1760.

SIR,

The command I have received from his Majesty, to pursue the war in this country, has determined me, if possible, to complete the companies of Rangers that were on foot last campaign; and as Capt. Wait called upon me yesterday, and represented that he could easily complete the one he commands in the colony of Connecticut and the Province of Massachuset's Bay, I have furnished him with beating orders for that purpose, as also with a warrant for 800 dollars on account of that service.

This day I have wrote to Capt. John Stark in New Hampshire, and Capt. David Brewer in the Massachuset's Bay, inclosing to each of them a beating order for the respective provinces; and I herewith send you a copy of the instructions that accompany the same, by which you will see they are ordered, as fast as they get any number of men, to send them to Albany. I am, Sir,

Your humble servant,

To Major Rogers.   Jeff Amherst.

My answer to the above:

★ *My own sley was taken with £1196 York currency in cash, besides stores and other neccessaries; £800 of this money belonging to the crown, which was afterwards allowed me, the remaining £396 was my own, which I entirely lost.*

Sir,

I received your Excellency's letter, dated the 1st instant, together with a copy of your instructions to Capt. John Stark and Capt. David Brewer, whereby I learn that they are to be at Albany by the 1st of May next with their companies. Since I received intelligence from your Excellency that the Rangers are to be raised again, I have wrote to several of my friends in New England, who will assist them in compleating their companies; and as many of the men belonging to the two companies here were frost-bitten in the winter, and others sick, many of whom I judged would not be fit for service the ensuing campaign, I employed Lieut. McCormack, of Capt. William Stark's company (that was with Major Scott) Lieut. John Fletcher, and one Holmes, and sent them recruiting the 20th of February for my own and Captain Johnson's company, and advanced them 1100 dollars. These three recruiters I do not doubt will bring in good men enough to complete us here; so that those who are frost-bitten may be sent to hospitals, and those unfit for duty discharged, or otherwise disposed of, as your Excellency shall direct.

There being so few Rangers fit for duty here, and those that are much wanted at this place, has prevented me from proposing any tour of the French and Indian settlements in pursuit of a prisoner, which may, I believe, be easily got at this time, if sent for. I am Sir,

Your Excellency's most obedient humble sevant,

R. Rogers

To General Amherst.

A letter from General Amherst:

SIR,

As I have not heard that either of the Jacobuses, who each commanded a company of Stockbridge Indians the last campaign, are returned from their captivity, I would have you write (if you think Lieut. Solomon capable of and fit for such a command) to him, to know if he chuses to accept of the same; but it must be upon condition of bringing to the field none but good men, that are well inclined, and that are hale and strong. Whatever number he or any of his friends can raise that will answer this description, I will readily employ this summer, and they shall meet with all the encouragement their services shall merit. All others that are too old or too young, I shall reject, nor shall I make them any allowance of payment, altho' they should join the army; so that, in order to prevent his having any difference with these people, it will behove him to engage none but what shall be esteemed fit for the service; he must also observe to be assembled with them at Albany by the 1st of May at furthest, from which day he and they shall be enlisted to their pay, that is, for so many as shall be mustered there, and for no more; he must likewise take care that every man comes provided with a good firelock, and that they be always ready to march at a moment's warning, wherever they are ordered to, in default of which they shall forfeit their pay that shall be due them at that time. All this you will explain to him particularly, and so soon as you receive his answer, inform me thereof. As an encouragement to enter the service upon the foregoing conditions, you may assure him also, that if he conforms to them in every respect, and that he and his men prove useful, they shall be better rewarded than they have yet been.

Capt. Ogden having solicited me for a company of

Rangers, assured me that he could raise and complete a very good one in the Jersies; I gave him a beating order for that purpose, and instructions similar to those I sent you a copy of in my last for Captains Stark and Brewer, and have also granted him a warrant for five hundred dollars, on account of the bounty-money, to be as usual stopped out of the first warrant for the subsistence of that company. I am, Sir,

Your humble servant,

To Major Rogers.   *Jeff. Amherst.*

My Letter to the General.

Crown Point, 20th March, 1760.

SIR,

I observe the contents of your Excellency's letter of the 19th, and shall take particular care to let Lieut Solomon know every circumstance relative to his being employed the next summer, and to advise your Excellency as soon as I hear from him. He has already informed me he would be glad to engage with some Indians.

Mr. Stuart, the Adjutant of the Rangers, who is at Albany, I have desired to go to Stockbridge, to deliver Solomon his orders, and to explain them properly to him.

I am heartily glad that your excellency hath been pleased to give to Capt. Ogden a company of the Rangers, who, from the good character he bears, I doubt not will answer your expectations.

Inclosed is a sketch of my travels to and from St. Francis. I am, Sir,

Your Excellency's most humble servant,

To General Amherst.   *R. Rogers.*

The General's letter to me.

New York, 6th April, 1760.

SIR,

I am to own the receipt of your letters of the 15th and 20th ultimo, and to approve what you therein mention to have done for completing your and Capt. Johnson's company; as also your having sent Adjutant Stuart to Stockbridge, to deliver Solomon his orders, and to explain them properly to him. This will avoid all mistakes, and enable you the sooner to inform me of Solomon's intentions, which I shall be glad to know as soon as possible.

I thank you for your sketch of your travels to and from St. Francis, and am, Sir,

Your very humble servant,

To Major Rogers.   *Jeff. Amherst.*

Soon after this I had the pleasure of informing the General that the Stockbridge Indians determined to enter the service this year; but as many of them were out a hunting, that they could not be collected at Albany before the 10th of May; and that the recruits of the ranging companies began to assemble at Crown Point.

May 4, 1760

This day Serjeant Beverly, who had been taken prisoner, and made his escape, came in seven days from Montreal to Crown Point. He had lived at the Governor's (Monsieur de Vaudreuil) house, and brought the following intelligence, which I immediately transmitted to the General, viz.

"That about the 10th of April, the enemy withdrew all their troops from Nut Island, excepting 300, which they left there to garrison the place, under the command of Monsieur Bonville: that the enemy also brought from the island one half of the ammunition they had there, and half of the cannon: that the enemy had two frigates, one of 36 guns, the other of 20 guns, that lay all winter in the river St. Lawrence, and some other small vessels, such as row-galleys, &c. that all the troops of France in Canada went down to Jecorty the 20th April, except those left to garrison their fort, which was very slenderly done, together with all the militia that could be spared out of the country, leaving only one man to two females to sow their grain, where they were assembled by Monsieur Levy, their General, with an intent to retake Quebec*: that ninety six men of the enemy were drowned going down to Jecorty: that he saw a man who was taken prisoner the 15th of April, belonging to our troops at Quebec: that this man told him our garrison there was healthy; and that Brigadier General Murray had 4000 men fit for duty in the city, besides a post of 300 men at Point Levy, which the

*This place, the capital of all Canada, had been taken by the English troops last year, under the command of General Wolfe.

131

enemy attempted to take possession of in the month of February last, with a considerable body of troops, and began to fortify a church at or near the Point, but that General Murray sent over a detachment of about 1000 men, which drove the enemy from their post, and took a Captain, with about thirty French soldiers, prisoners, and fortified the church for his own conveniency: that the General has another post on the north-side of the river at Laurat, a little distance from the town, in which he keeps 300 men: that there is a line of block-houses well fortified all roud the land-side of the town, under cover of the cannon: that a breast-work of fraziers is extended from one block-house to another, as far as those houses extend: that they heard at Quebec of the enemy's coming, but were not in the least concerned: that a detachment from Quebec surprised two of the enemy's guards, at a place called Point de Treamble, each guard consisting of fifty men, and killed or took the most part of them. One of those guards were all grenadiers."

He moreover reports:

"That two more of our frigates had got up the river, and that two more men of war were near the Island of Orleans: that the French told him that there was a fleet of ten sail of men of war seen at Gaspee Bay, with some transports, but put back to sea again on account of the ice; but as they had up different colours, they could not tell whether they were French or English: that the beginning of May the enemy was to draw off 2000 of their men to Nut Island, and as many more to Oswagotchy: he heard that they did not intend to attack Quebec, except the French fleet gets up the river before ours: that 100 Indians were to come this way, and set out about the fifth of May; the remainder of the Indians were at present gone to Jecorty: that Gen. Levy, the Attawawas, and Cold Country Indians, will all be in Canada by the beginning of June, ten sachems being sent by the French last fall, to call those nations to their assistance: that a great number had deserted to the French from the battalion of Royal Americans at Quebec, which the French have engaged in their service; but that they were to be sent off, under the care of Monsieur Boarbier, up to Attawawas River, to the French colony betwixt the lakes and the Mississippi River: that the most part of the enemy's Indians are intent on going there; and that a great number of French, especially those who have money, think to save it by carrying it to New Orleans: that he saw at Montreal two Rangers, Reynolds and Hall, that were returned by Col. Haviland deserted last fall: that they were taken prisoners near River-head Block-house, when after cattle: that two more Rangers are to be here in ten days with fresh intelligence from Montreal, if they can possibly make their escape: that Monsieur Longee, the famous partisan, was drowned in the river St. Laurence, a few days after he returned with the party that took Capt. Tute: that the Indians have a great eye to the No. 4. roads, as they say they can get sheep and oxen coming here from that place: that he heard Gen. Murray had hanged several Canadians lately, that were carrying ammunition out of Quebec to the enemy: that the two Captains Jacobs are still in Canada; the one taken with Capt. Kennedy is on board a vessel in irons, the other ran away last fall, but returned, having froze his feet, and is at Montreal."

A few days after this, I went down the Lake Champlain, to reconnoitre Nut Island, and the garrison there, the landing places, &c. On my return from that service to Crown Point, I had an order from Gen. Amherst to repair to Albany, the head-quarters, as fast as possible.

I set out, in obedience to this order, the 18th of May, and

waited upon the General at Albany the 23rd, and gave him all the information I could, in regard to the passage into Canada by the Island de Noix, or Nut Island, and likewise that by Oswego and La Galette.

The General being acquainted by an express, that Quebec was then besieged by the French, informed me of his intentions of sending me with a party into Canada, and if the siege of Quebec was continued, to destroy their country as far as possible, and by constantly marching from one place to another, try to draw off the enemy's troops, and prolong the siege till our vessels got up the river. He strongly recommended, and ordered me to govern myself according to the motions of the French army; to retreat if they had raised the siege; and in case, by prisoners or otherwise, I should find the siege still going on, to harrass the country, tho' it were at the expence of my party. I had at the same time thefollowing instructions from him in writing:

Major Rogers, you are to take under your command a party of 300 men, composed of 275 Rangers, with their proper officers, and a subaltern, two serjeants and twenty-five men of the Light Infantry regiments; with which detachment you will proceed down the lake, under convoy of the brig, where you will fix upon the safest and best place for laying up your boats, which I imagine one of the islands will best answer, while you are executing the following services.

You will with 250 men land on the west-side, in such manner that you may get to St. John's (without the enemy at the Isle au Noix having any intelligence of it) where you will try to surprize the fort, and destroy the vessels, boats, provisions, or whatever else may be there for the use of the troops at the Isle au Noix. You will then march to Fort Chamblé, where you will do the same, and you will destroy every magazine you can find in that part, so as to distress the enemy as much as you can. This will soon be known at the Isle au Noix, and you must take care not to be cut off in your retreat; for which reason, when you have done all you think practicable on the western-side, I judge your best and safest retreat will be, to cross the river and march back the east-side of Isle au Noix. When you land on the west-side, you will send such officer with the fifty Rangers, as you think will best answer their intended service, which is, to march for Wigwam Martinique, to destroy what he may find there and on the east side of the river, and afterwards to join you, or to retreat in such manner as you will direct him. You will take such provisions as you judge necessary with you, and fix with Capt. Grant (who shall have orders to wait for your return) the places where he may look out for you when you come back.

You will take your men as light with you as possible, and give them all the necessary caution for the conduct, and their obedience to their officers; no firing without order, no unneccessary alarms, no retreating without an order; they are to stick by one another and nothing can hurt them; let every man whose firelock will carry it have a bayonet; you are not to suffer the Indians to destroy women or children, no plunder to be taken to load your men, who shall be rewarded at their return as they deserve.

May 25, 1760.   *Jeff. Amherst.*

With the above instructions the General delivered me a letter directed to General Murray at Quebec, desiring me to convey it to him in such manner as I thought would be quickest and safest.

Having received these instructions I returned to Crown Point as fast as possible, and about the beginning of June set out from thence with a party of two hundred and fifty men*

*The Stockbridge Indians who had been mustered at, and now marched from Albany, and who were to be a part of the detachment of 300, agreeable to the General's orders, had not arrived at Crown Point at the time of my embarkation, but were ordered to follow after and join me.

down Lake Champlain, having four vessels, on board of which this detachment embarked, putting our boats and provisions into them, that the enemy might have less opportunity of discovering our designs.

The 3d, I landed Lieut. Holmes with fifty men in Misisquey Bay, and gave him proper directions agreeable to my orders from the General, informing him that one of the sloops should cruise for him till his return, which upon signals that were given him would take him on board, upon which he was to join me or wait on board till my return, as the situation of affairs might direct him. Here likewise I sent the letter I had received from the General to Brigadier Murray, thro' the woods, and gave the following instructions to the officer I intrusted with it viz.

Instructions for Serjeant Beverly of his Majesty's Rangers.

You are hereby directed to take under your command, these three men, viz. John Shute, Luxford Goodwin, and Joseph Eastman, and march them from Misisquey Bay, to which place you will be convoyed by Lieut. Holmes with a party I have sent there for a particular purpose; you are to land in the night-time, as otherwise you may be discovered by a party from the Isle au Noix; you will steer your course about north-east, and make all the dispatch you possibly can with the letter in your charge to Quebec, or to the English army at or near that place, and deliver it to Brigadier Murray, or to the officer commanding his Majesty's forces in or upon the river St. Lawrence. A sketch of the country will be delivered you with these orders, that you may the better know the considerable rivers you have to cross, betwixt Misisquey Bay and Quebec. The distances are marked in the draught, as is the road I travelled in last fall, from Misisquey Bay to St. Francis, which road you will cross several times, if you keep the course I before directed. The rivers are so plainly described in the plan, that you will know them when you come to them. The river St. Francis is about half-way of your journey, and is very still water, and may be easily rafted where you cross it; but lower down it is so swift and rapid that you must not attempt it. Shedoir River you will likewise be obliged to pass on a raft; it is swift water for some miles from its mouth; you had better examine it well before you attempt to cross it. As soon as you pass this river, steer your course about east, leaving Point Levy on your left hand, and fall in with the river St. Lawrence, near the lower end of the iland of Orleans, as it may be possible that Gen. Murray may have encamped the army either at the isle of Orleans or the isle of Quodoa; therefore you are not to depend on finding at once the exact place of his encampment, but are positively to look out for the English fleet, and the first line of battle ship you see, you are to venture on board, as I think it not possible the enemy should have any large ships there, and whatever English ship you get on board of, will convoy you directly to General Murray, when you will deliver him the verbal message I told you. You may apply to the General for fifty pounds, who will pay it to you, and also give you proper directions to join me as soon as you have rested yourself from your march. I wish you a good journey, and am,

Your's, &c.

To Serjeant Beverley,   *Robert Rogers.*

As soon as I had dispatched the two parties before-mentioned, I, with the remainder, crossed Lake Champlain to the west-side, and the 4th in the morning got into my boats, and landed with about 200 men, about twelve miles south of the island Noix, with an intent to put in execution the General's orders to me of May 5th with all speed. Capt. Grant sent the two sloops to attend, which I ordered to cruize further down the lake than where I landed, and nearer to their fort, to command the attention of the enemy till I could get into their country. I lay still all the 5th, there being a heavy rain, and the bushes so wet that both we and our provisions would have been greatly exposed by a march.

In the afternoon of this day, several French boats appeared on the Lake, which were discovered by the two sloops, as well as by my party on the shore. These boats continued as near as they could to our vessels without endangering themselves, till after dark. Concluding their boats would cruize the whole night to watch the motions of our sloops, I imagined it would be a prudent step to send the sloops back to Capt. Grant, the commander of these vessels, who lay near Mott Island; I accordingly went to the sloops in a boat after dark, and ordered them to return.

The enemy, who kept all night in their boats, having, by a strict look-out, discovered where I landed, sent a detachment from the island next morning to cut off my party. I discovered their intentions by my reconnoitering parties, who counted them as they crossed from the fort in the morning in their boats, to the west-shore, and informed me that they were 350 in number. I had intelligence again that they were about a mile from us. Half after eleven they attacked me very briskly on my left, having on my right a bog, which they did not venture over, thro' which, however, by the edge of the lake, I sent seventy of my party to get round and attack them in the rear.

This party was commanded by Lieut. Farrington. As soon as he began his attack, I pushed them in front, which broke them immediately. I pursued them with the greatest part of my people about a mile, where they retired to a thick cedar swamp, and divided into small parties. By this time it rained again very hard. I called my party immediately together at the boats, where I found that Ensign Wood of the 17th regiment was killed, Capt. Johnson wounded through the body, a second shot through his left arm, and a third in his head. I had two men of the Light Infantry, and eight Rangers, wounded, and sixteen Rangers killed. We killed forty of the enemy, and recovered about fifty firelocks. Their commanding officer, Monsieur la Force, was mortally hurt, and several of the party were likewise wounded.

After the action I got the killed and maimed of my detachment together in battoes, returned with them to the Isle à Mot, near which the brig lay. I dispatched one of the vessels to Crown Point, on board of which was put the corpse of Mr. Wood, but Capt. Johnson died on his passage thither; this vessel I ordered to bring more provisions. I buried the rest of the dead on an island, and then began to prepare for a second landing; being joined about this time by the Stockbridge Indian Company, I was determined at all adventures to pursue my orders, settled the plan of landing, and left the following instructions with Capt. Grant, viz.

You will be so good as to fall down the lake with your vessels as soon as possible, as far as the Wind Mill Point, or near where you lay at anchor the last time I was with you, and cruize near it for two or three days, which will be the only method I can think of that has any appearance of attracting the attention of the enemy till I get into their country; as soon as I observe or think you pretty near the Wind Mill Point, I shall land with my party on the west-side opposite to the north-end of the Isle a Mot, in the river that runs into the bay which forms itself there, and from thence proceed to execute the General's orders. If they do not attack me in my march till I compleat my design, you may be certain I shall come back to the east-side, and endeavour to join you near the Wind Mill Point, or betwixt that and the Isle à Mot. When I arrive, the signal that I will make for your discovering me, will be a smoak and three guns, at three minute's interval each from the other, and repeated a second time, in half an hour after the first; but if the enemy should attack me on my march before I get to the place I am ordered, which I believe they will do, in case I am worsted I shall be obliged to come back on the west-side, and shall make the before mentioned signals betwixt the Isle à Mot and the place where I had the battle with the enemy the 6th instant. It is uncertain when I shall be at either shore; so that I would recommend it to you not to come back south of the Isle á Mot till my return, as a contrary wind might prevent your getting in with your vessels to relieve me. I send you Serjeant Hackett and ten Rangers, to be with you in my absence, as we this day agreed. If Lieutenant Darcy comes down in season to go with me, I shall leave Ensign Wilson with you; but if Darcy should not come till after I land, you'll be pleased to take him under your direction, as well as those that may come with him to join me; tho' I would recommend it not to send any party to the island, to take a prisoner, till the fifth day after my landing, as the loss of a man from us may be of very bad consequence. Lieutenant Holmes has appointed between the eleventh and sixteenth day after his landing for his return to Misisquey Bay, and from the eleventh to the sixteenth, as before mentioned; I should be glad the sloop might cruize for him at the place he appointed to meet her. I am, SIR,

Your humble servant,

R. Rogers.

I cannot but observe with pleasure, that Mr. Grant, like an able officer, very diligently did all that could be expected of him for the good of the service, carefully attending with his vessels till my return from this second excursion, on which I embarked with two hundred and twenty men, officers included, and landed the 9th of June about midnight on the west-shore opposite the Isle à Mot, from thence marched as fast as possible to St. John's, and came to the road that leads from it to Montreal, about two miles from the fort, the evening of the 15th.

At eleven o'clock this night, I marched with an intent to surprise the fort, to within four hundred yards of it, where I halted to reconnoitre; which I did, and found they had more men than I expected. The number of the centries within the fort were seventeen, and so well fixed, that I thought it was impossible for me to take the place by surprise, especially as they had seen me, and fired several guns accordingly.

I left it at two o'clock, and marched down the river to St. d'Etrese; at break of day I reconnoitred this place, and found that the enemy had in it a stockaded fort, defensible against small arms. I observed two large store-houses in the inside, and that the enemy were carting hay into the fort.

I waited for an opportunity when the cart had just entered the gate-way, run forward, and got into the fort before they could clear the way for shutting the gate. I had at this time sent different parties to the several houses, about fifteen in number, which were near the fort, and were all surprised at the same instant of time, and without firing a single gun.

We took in the fort twenty-four soldiers, and in the houses seventy-eight prisoners, women and children included; some young men made their escape to Chamblee.

I examined the prisoners, and found I could not proceed to Chamblee with any prospect of success, therefore concluded my best way was to burn the fort and village, which I did, together with a considerable magazine of hay, and some provisions, with every battoe and canoe, except eight battoes which I kept to cross the river, and these we afterwards cut to pieces: we also killed their cattle, horses, &c. destroyed their waggons, and every other thing which we thought could ever be of service to the enemy. When this was done, I sent back the women and children, and gave them a pass to go to Montreal, directed to the several officers of the different detachments under my command. I continued my march on the east-side of Lake Champlain, and when passing by Misisquey Bay, opposite the Isle Noix, my advance-party, and the advance-party of about 800 French, that were out after me from their fort, engaged with each other; but the body of the enemy, being about a mile behind their advance-party, retreated, to my great satisfaction.

I pursued my march with all possible speed: and the same day, being the 20th day of June, arrived at the lake opposite where the vessels lay; and as I had sent a few men forward to repeat the signals, the boats met us at the shore. We directly put on board, the enemy soon after appeared on the shore where we embarked. I had not at this time any account from Lieutenant Holmes, either by prisoners or otherways.

Upon examination the prisoners reported, (some of them had been at the siege of Quebec) "that the French lost five hundred men there; and that they retreated after twelve days bombarding and cannonading, and came to Jack's quarters, where General Levy left five hundred men, being composed of a picquet of each battalion of the army, and that there were four hundred Canadians who staid voluntarily with them; that the rest of the army was quartered by two's and three's on the inhabitants, from there to St. John's. In Montreal there are about a hundred and fifty troops, and the inhabitants do duty. That in Chamblee Fort are about one hundred and fifty men, including workmen; and the remnant of the Queen's regiment are in the village. That there are twelve cannon at St John's, and about three hundred men, including workmen, who are obliged to take arms on any alarm. That at the Isle au Noix are about eight hundred stationed, besides the scouts between that and Montreal. That there are about an hundred pieces of cannon there." This is the substance of their report, in which they all agree, and which, with an account of my proceedings, I transmitted to the General.

On the 21st I put the twenty-six prisoners on board one of the vessels, with fifty men of my detachment, and ordered her to proceed to Crown point, and tarried with the other vessels to Cover Mr. Holmes's retreat, who joined us the same evening, without having succeeded in his enterprise, missing his way by following down a river that falls into Sorrel, instead of that called Wigwam Macinac, which empties itself into St. Lawrence at Lake St. Francis. I arrived at Crown Point the 23rd of June, and encamped my Rangers on the east-shore, opposite the fort.

The following letter I received from General Amherst, dated Canijoharry, June 26, 1760.

SIR,

Colonel Haviland sent me your letter of June 21, which I received last night, and saw with pleasure you was returned without the loss of a man in your party, and that you had done every thing that was prudent for you to attempt with the number of men you had under your command. From the situation the enemy is now in, by being forced back to their former quarters, on Governor Murray's having obliged them to abandon their cannon, and raise the siege of Quebec, I hope Lieutenant Holmes will return with equal success as you have done, I am, Sir,

Your humble servant,

To Major Rogers.   *Jeff. Amherst.*

I remained at Crown point with my people, without effecting anything considerable, more than in small parties reconnoitring the country about the fort, while every thing was got in readiness for embarking the army the 16th of August; which was done accordingly, having one brig, three sloops, and four rideaus, which latter were occupied by the royal train of artillery, commanded by Lieut. Colonel Ord. Our order of march was as follows, viz.

Six hundred Rangers and seventy Indians in whale-boats in the front, commanded by Major Rogers, as an advance-guard for the whole army, all in a line a-breast, about half a mile a-head of the main body, followed by the light infantry and grenadiers in two columns, two boats a-breast in each column, commanded by Col. Darby. The right wing was composed of provincials, commanded by Brigadier Ruggles, who was second in command of the whole army. The left was made up of New Hampshire and Boston troops, commanded by Col. Thomas. The seventeenth and twenty-seventh regiments, with some few of the Royals, that formed the center column, were commanded by Major Campbell of the 17th regiment. Col. Haviland was in the front of these divisions, between that and the light infantry and grenadiers. The royal artillery followed the columns, and was commanded by Colonel Ord, who had, for his escort, one Rhode Island regiment of provincials. The sutlers, &c. followed the artillery.

In this manner we rowed down the lake forty miles the first day, putting ashore where there was good landing on the west-side, and there encamped.

The day following we lay by. The 18th, the wind blowing fresh at south, orders were given for embarking, and the same day reached a place on the west-shore, within ten miles of the Isle à Mot, where the army encamped. It having blown a fresh gale most part of the day, some of my boats split open by the violence of the waves, and ten of my Rangers were thereby drowned.

The 19th we set sail again early in the morning, and that night encamped on the north-end of the Isle à Mot.

The 20th, before day, the army was under way, with intention to land; having but twenty miles to go, and having the advantage of a fair wind, we soon came in sight of the French fort, and about ten in the morning Col. Darby, with the Grenadiers and Light Infantry, and myself with the Rangers, landed on the east-shore, and marched and took possession of the ground opposite the fort on that side, without the least opposition. Having done this, an officer was sent to acquaint

Col. Haviland (who, with the remainder of the army, was at the place where we landed) that there was not the least danger to apprehend from the enemy.

The next day we began to raise batteries, and soon after to throw some shells into the garrison. About the 24th a proposal was made for taking the enemy's vessels, three of which were at anchor a little below the fort, and some of their rideaus likewise. It was introduced by Col. Darby, who was ordered to take the command of the party appointed for this service, which consisted of two companies of Regulars, and four companies of my Rangers, with the Indians.

We carried with us two light hobitzers and one six-pounder, and silently conveying them along thro' the trees, brought them opposite the vessels, and began a brisk fire upon them, before they were in the least apprised of our design, and, by good fortune, the first shot from the six-pounder cut the cable of the great rideau, and the wind being at west, blew her to the east-shore, where we were, and the other vessels weighed anchor and made for St. John's, but got all a-ground, in turning a point about two miles below the fort.

I was, by Col. Darby, ordered down the east-shore with my Rangers, and crossed a river of about thirty yards wide, which falls into Lake Champlain from the east. I soon got opposite the vessels, and, by firing from the shore, gave an opportunity to some of my party to swim on board with their tomahawks, and took one of the vessels; in the mean time Col. Darby had got on board the rideau, and had her manned, and took the other two; of which success he immediately acquainted Col. Haviland, who sent down a sufficient number of men to take charge of and man the vessels; and ordered the remainder of the Rangers, Light Infantry and Grenadiers, to join the army that night, which was accordingly done; and about midnight the night following the French troops left the island, and landed safe on the main; so that next morning nothing of them was to be seen but a few sick, and Col. Haviland took possession of the fort.

The second day after the departure of Monsieur Bonville and his troops from the island, Mr. Haviland sent me with my Rangers to pursue him as far as St John's fort, which was about twenty miles further down the lake, and at that place I was to wait the coming of the army, but by no means to follow further than that fort, nor run any risk of advancing further towards Montreal. I went in boats, and about day-light got to St. John's, and found it just set on fire. I pursued, and took two prisoners, who reported, "That Monsieur Bonville was to encamp that night about half-way on the road to Montreal; and that he went from St. John's about nine o'clock the night before; but that many of their men were sick, and that they thought some of the troops would not reach the place appointed till the middle of the afternoon."

It being now about seven in the morning, I set all hands to work, except proper guards, to fortify the loghouses that stood near the lake-side, in order that part of my people might cover the battoes, while I, with the remainder, followed Monsieur Bonville, and about eight o'clock I got so well fortified, that I ventured our boats and baggage under the care of 200 Rangers, and took with me 400, together with the two companies of Indians, and followed after the French army, which consisted of about 1500 men, and about 100 Indians they had to guard them.

I was resolved to make this dance a little the merrier, and pursued with such haste, that I overtook his rear-guard about two miles before they got to their encamping ground. I immediately attacked them, who, not being above 200, suddenly broke, and then stood for the main body, which I very eagerly pursued, but in good order, expecting Monsieur Bonville would have made a stand, which however he did not chuse, but pushed forward to get to the river, where they were to encamp, and having crossed it, pulled up the bridge, which put a stop to my march, not judging it prudent to cross at a disadvantage, inasmuch as the enemy had a good breast-work on the other side, of which they took possession; in this pursuit, however, we considerably lessened their number, and returned in safety.

In the evening Mr. Haviland came in sight, and landed at St. John's. As soon as he came on shore, I waited upon him, and acquainted him with what I had done, &c. and that I had two prisoners for him; he said it was very well, and ordered his troops to encamp there that night, and next day went down the river Sorriel, as far as St. d'Etrese, where he encamped, and made a strong breast-work, to defend his people from being surprised. I was sent down the river Sorriel, to bring the inhabitants under subjection to his Britannic Majesty, and went into their settled country in the night, took all their priests and militia officers, and sent some of them for the inhabitants.

The first day I caused all the inhabitants near Chamblee to take the oaths of allegiance, &c. who appeared glad to have it in their power to take the oaths and keep their possessions, and were all extremely submissive. Having obliged them to bring in their arms, and fulfilled my instructions in the best manner I could, I joined Col. Darby at Chamblee, who came there to take the fort, and had brought with him some light cannon. It soon surrendered, as the garrison consisted only of about fifty men. This happened on the first of September.

On the 2d, our army having nothing to do, and having good intelligence both from Gen. Amherst and Gen. Murray, Mr. Haviland sent me to join the latter, while he marched with the rest of the army for La Pierre. The 5th in the morning I got to Longville, about four miles below Montreal, opposite where Brigadier Murray lay, and gave him notice of my arrival, but not till the morning of the 6th, by reason of my arriving so late.

By the time I came to Longville, the army, under the command of Gen. Amherst, had landed about two miles from the town, where they encamped; and early this morning

Monsieur de Vaudreuil, the governor and commander in chief of all Canada, sent out to capitulate with our General, which put a stop to all our movements till the 8th of September, when the articles of capitulation were agreed to, and signed, and our troops took possession of the town-gates that night. Next morning the Light Infantry, and Grenadiers of the whole army, under the command of Col. Haldiman, with a company of the royal artillery, with two pieces of cannon, and some hobitzers, entered the town, retaking the English colours belonging to Pepperel's and Shirley's regiments, which had been taken by the French at Oswego.

Thus, at length, at the end of the fifth campaign, Montreal and the whole country of Canada was given up, and became subject to the King of Great Britain; a conquest perhaps of the greatest importance that is to be met with in the British annals, whether we consider the prodigious extent of country we are hereby made masters of, the vast addition it must make to trade and navigation, or the security it must afford to the northern provinces of America, particularly those flourishing ones of New England and New York, the irretrievable loss France sustains hereby, and the importance it must give the British crown among the several states of Europe: all this, I say, duly considered, will, perhaps, in its consequences render the year 1760 more glorious than any preceding.

And to this acquisition, had we, during the late war, either by conquest or treaty, added the fertile and extensive country of Louisiana, we should have been possessed of perhaps the most valuable territory upon the face of the globe, attended with more real advantages than the so-much-boasted mines of Mexico and Peru, and would have for ever deprived the French, those treacherous rivals of Britain's glory, of an opportunity of acting hereafter the same perfidious parts they have already so often repeated.

On the 9th Gen. Amherst informed me of his intention of sending me to Detroit, and on the 12th in the morning, when I waited upon him again, I received the following orders:

By his Excellency Jeffery Amherst, Esq;
Major General and Commander in Chief of all his
Majesty's forces in North America &c. &c. &c.

To Major Rogers, commanding his Majesty's
independant companies of Rangers.

You will, upon receipt hereof, with Capt. Waite's and Capt. Hazen's companies of Rangers under your command, proceed in whale-boats from hence to Fort William-Augustus, taking along with you one Joseph Poupao, alias La Fleur, an inhabitant of Detroit, and Lieut. Brehme, Assistant Engineer.

From Fort William-Augustus you will continue your voyage by the north-shore to Niagara, where you will land your whale-boats, and transport them across the Carrying-place into Lake Erie, applying to Major Walters, or the officer commanding at Niagara, for any assistance you may want on that or any other occasion, requesting of him at the same time to deliver up to you Monsieur Gamelin, who was made prisoner at the reduction of said fort, and has continued there ever since, in order to conduct him, with the above mentioned Poupao, to their habitations at Detroit, where, upon taking the oath of allegiance to his most sacred Majesty, whose subjects they are become by the capitulation of the 8th instant; they shall be protected in the peacable and quiet possession of their properties, and, so long as they behave as becometh good and faithful subjects, shall partake of all the other privileges and immunities granted unto them by the said capitulation.

With these, and the detachment under your command, you will proceed in your whale-boats across Lake Erie to Presque Isle, where, upon your arrival, you will make known the orders I have given to the officer commanding that post; and you will leave said whale-boats and party, taking only a small detachment of your party, and marching by land, to join Brigadier General Monkton, wherever he may be.

Upon your arrival with him, you will deliver into his hands the dispatches you shall herewith receive for him, and follow and obey such orders as he shall give you for the relief of the garrisons of the French posts at Detroit, Michlimakana, or any others in that district, for gathering in the arms of the inhabitants thereof, and for administering to them the oath of allegiance already mentioned; when you will likewise administer, or see administered, the same to the before-mentioned Gamelin and Poupao; and when this is done, and that you have reconnoitered and explored the country as much as you can, without losing time unneccessarily, you are to bring away the French troops and arms, to such place as you shall be directed by Gen. Monkton.

And when the whole of this service is compleated, you will march back your detachment to Presque Isle, or Niagara, according to the orders you receive from Brigadier Monkton, where you will embark the whole, and in like manner, as before, transport your whale-boats across the Carrying-place, into Lake Ontario, where you will deliver over your whale-boats into the care of the commanding officer, marching your detachment by land to Albany, or wherever I may be, to receive what further orders I may have to give you.

Given under my hand, at the head quarters in the camp of Montreal, 12th Sept. 1760.

Jeff. Amherst.

By his Excellency's command,

J. Appy.

An additional order was given, which was to be shewn only to the commanding officers of the different posts I might touch at, the expedition being intended to be kept a profound secret, for fear the march should be impeded by the enemy Indians, through whose country I was obliged to march. This order was as follows, viz:

Major Walters, or the officer commanding at Niagara, will judge whether or not there is provision sufficient at Presque Isle; and Major Rogers will accordingly take provisions from Niagara. Eight days provision will take him from Montreal to Fort William-Augustus; there he will apply to the commanding officer for a sufficient quantity to proceed to Niagara. Major Rogers knows where he is going, and the provisions he will want; some should be in store likewise at Presque Isle, for the party Brigadier Monkton will send.

Jeff. Amherst.

Montreal, 12th Sept. 1760.

In pursuance of these orders I embarked at Montreal the 13th Sept. 1760 (with Captain Brewer, Captain Wait, Lieutenant Brheme, Assistant Engineer, Lieut. Davis of the royal train of artillery, and two hundred Rangers) about noon, in fifteen whale-boats; and that night we encamped at la Chine; next morning we reached Isle de Praires, and took a view of the two Indian settlements of Coyhavagu and Conesadagu.

On the 16th we got up to an island in the Lake St. Francis, and the next night encamped on the western shore, at the lower end of the upper rifts. We ascended these rifts the day following, and continued all night on the north-shore, opposite a number of islands.

In the evening of the 19th we came to the Isle de Gallettes, and spent the 20th in repairing our whale-boats, which had received some damage in ascending the rifts.

This morning I sent off ten sick Rangers to Albany, by the way of Oswego, recommending them to the care of Col. Fitch, commanding at Oswego, who was to give them suitable directions.

We left Isle de Gallettes on the 21st; about twelve o'clock, the wind being unfavourable, we passed Oswegachi, and encamped but three miles above it on the northern shore.

On the 22nd we continued our course up the river, the wind blowing fresh at south, and halted in the evening at the narrow passes near the islands; but, upon the wind's abating at midnight, we embarked and rowed the remainder of that night, and the whole day following, till we came to the place where formerly stood the old Fort of Frontiniac, where we found some Indian hunters from Oswegachi. We were detained here all the next day by the tempestuousness of the weather, which was very windy, attended with snow and rain; we, however, improved the time in taking a plan of the old fort, situated at the bottom of a fine safe harbour.

There were about five hundred acres of cleared ground about it, which, tho' covered with clover, seemed bad and rocky, and interspersed with some pine-trees. The Indians here seemed to be well pleased with the news we brought them of the surrender of all Canada, and supplied us with great plenty of venison and wild fowl.

We left this place the 25th, about ten in the morning, steering a south-course two miles, then west six miles, which brought us to the mouth of a river thirty feet wide; then south four miles, where we halted to refresh the party.

About four in the afternoon we rowed for a mountain bearing south-west, which we did not come up to till some time in the night, and found it to be a steep rock, about one hundred feet high. It now grew foggy, and mistaking our way about six miles, we rowed all night, and till 8 o'clock next morning, before we put ashore; which we then did on a point, where we breakfasted, and then proceeded on our voyage, rowing till 8 o'clock at night (being about one hundred miles, as we imagined, from Frontiniac) we landed. This evening we passed two small islands at the end of a point extending far into the lake; the darkness and fog prevented us from taking such a survey of them as to be able to give a particular description of them.

September 27, 1760

Being very windy, we spent the time in deer-hunting, there being great plenty of them there, tho' the land is rocky, the timber bad, chiefly hemlock and pine; and I believe it is generally so on the north-side of Lake Ontario.

We embarked very early on the 28th, steering south-west, leaving a large bay on the right, about twenty miles wide; the western side of which terminates in a point, and a small island: having passed both, about fifteen miles on a course west by south, we entered the chops of a river, called by the Indians the *Grace of Man*; there we encamped, and found about 50 Mississagua Indians fishing for salmon. At our first appearamnce they ran down, both men and boys, to the edge of the lake, and continued firing their pieces, to express their joy at the sight of the English colours, till such time as we had landed.

They presented me with a deer just killed and split in halves, with the skin on, but the bowels taken out, which, with them, is a most elegant and polite present, and significant of the greatest respect. I told them of the success of their English brethren, against their fathers the French; at which they either were, or pretended to be, very well pleased.

Some of us fished with them in the evening, being invited by them, and filled a bark-canoe with salmon in about half an hour. Their method of catching the fish is very extraordinary. One person holds a lighted pine-torch, while a second strikes the fish with a spear. This is the season in which the salmon spawn in these parts, contrary to what they do in any other place I ever knew them before.

I found the soil near this river very good and level. The timber is chiefly oak and maple, or the sugar-tree.

At seven o'clock the next morning we took our departure from this river, the wind being a-head. About fifteen miles further, on a west-south-west course, we put into another river, called Life of Man. The Messissaguas, who were hunting here, about thirty in number, paid us the same compliments with those we just before received from their countrymen, and, instead of deer, split up a young bear, and presented me with it. Plenty of fish was catched here also. The land continued good and level, the soil of a blackish colour, and the banks of the lake were low.

The wind being fair the 30th, we embarked at the first dawn of day, and with the assistance of sails and oars, made great way on a south-west course, and in the evening reached the river Toronto, having run seventy miles. Many points extending far into the lake, occasioned a frequent alteration of our course. We passed a bank of twenty miles in length, but the land behind it seemed to be level, well-timbered with large oaks, hickaries, maples, and some poplars. No mountains appeared in sight. There was a track of about 300 acres of cleared ground, round the place where formerly the French had a fort, that was called Fort Toronto. The soil here is principally clay. The deer are extremely plenty in this country.

Some Indians were hunting at the mouth of the river, who run into the woods at our approach, very much frightened. They came in, however, in the morning, and testified their joy at the news of our success against the French. They told us that we could easily accomplish our journey from thence to Detroit in eight days: that when the French traded at that place, the Indians used to come with their poultry from Michlimakana, down the river Toronto: that the partage was but twenty miles from that to a river falling into Lake Huron, which had some falls, but none very considerable: they added, that there was a Carrying-place of fifteen miles from some westerly part of Lake Erie, to a river running without any falls, thro' several Indian towns into Lake St. Clair.

I think Toronto a most convenient place for a factory, and that from thence we may very easily settle the north-side of Lake Erie.

We left Toronto the 1st of October, steering south, right across the west-end of Lake Ontario. At dark we arrived at the south-shore, five miles west of Fort Niagara, some of our boats being now become exceeding leaky and dangerous.

This morning, before we set out, I directed the following order of march: "The boats in a line. If the wind rose high, the red flag hoisted, and the boats to crowd nearer, that they might be ready to give mutual assistance in case of a leak or other accident;" by which means we saved the crew and arms of the boat commanded by Lieut. M'Cormack, which sprung a leak and sunk, losing nothing except their packs.

We halted all the next day at Niagara, and provided ourselves with blankets, coats, shirts, shoes, magassins &c.

I received from the commanding officer eighty barrels of provisions, and changed two whale-boats for as many battoes, which proved leaky.

In the evening some of my party proceeded with the provisions to the falls, and in the morning marched the rest there, and began the portage of the provisions and boats. Mess. Brheme and Davis took a survey of the great cataract of Niagara.

As the winter-season was now advancing very fast in this country, and I had orders to join Brig. Monkton from Presque Isle, wherever he might be, to receive his directions, I set out this evening, the 5th of October, in a bark-canoe, with Lieutenants Brheme and Holmes, and eight Rangers, leaving the command of my party to Capt. Brewer, with instructions to follow to Presque Isle, and encamped eight miles up the stream issuing out of Lake Erie. The land appeared to be good on both sides of the river.

Next morning embarked early, and steered a south-west course. About noon opened Lake Erie, and leaving a bay to the left, we arrived by sun-set at the southern shore of the lake; we then steered west till eight o'clock at night, and drew up our boats on a sandy beach, forty miles distant from where we embarked in the morning.

The wind was very fresh next day, which prevented our setting out till 11 o'clock; so that we made no further progress than about twenty-eight miles on a west-south-west course. A little after noon, on the 8th of October, we arrived at Presque Isle, having kept a southerly course all the morning; I tarried there till 3 o'clock, when, having sent back my party to assist Capt. Brewer, Mr. Brheme, Lieutenant Holmes, and myself took leave of Colonel Bouquet, who commanded at Presque Isle, and with three other men, in a bark-canoe, proceeded to French Creek, and at night encamped on the road, half way to Fort du Bouf. We got to this fort about 10 o'clock next day, and after three hours rest launched our canoe into the river, and paddled down about ten miles below the fort.

On the 10th we encamped at the second crossings of the river, the land on both sides appeared to be good all the way. The 11th we reached Mingo Cabbins, and the night of the 12th we lodged at Venango; from thence went down the River Ohio; and on the morning of the 17th I waited upon Brigadier Monkton at Pittsburgh, and delivered him General Amherst's dispatches, and my own instructions.

I left Pittsburgh the 20th, at the request of General Monkton, who promised to send his orders after me to Presque Isle, by Mr. Croghan, and to forward Capt. Campbell immediately with a company of the Royal Americans; I got back to Presque Isle the 30th of October, Captain Campbell arrived the day after; Captain Brewer was got there before us, with the Rangers from Niagara, having lost some of the boats, and part of the provisions.

We immediately began to repair the damaged boats; and, as there was an account that a vessel, expected with provisions from Niagara, was lost, I dispatched Capt. Brewer by land to

Detroit, with a drove of forty oxen, supplied by Col. Bouquet. Capt. Wait was about the same time sent back to Niagara for more provisions, and ordered to cruise along the north-coast of Lake Erie, and halt about twenty miles to the east of the streight between the Lakes Huron and Erie, till further orders. Brewer had a battoe to ferry his party over the Creeks, two horses, and Capt. Monter with twenty Indians, composed of the Six Nations, Delawares, and Shawnese, to protect him from the insults of the enemy Indians.

My order of march over from Presque Isle was as follows:

The boats to row two deep; first, Major Rogers's boat, abreast with him Capt. Croghan; Capt Campbell follows with his company, the Rangers next, and lastly, Lieutenant Holmes, who commands the rear-guard, with his own boat, and that of Ensign Wait's, so as to be able to assist any boat that may be in distress. Boats in distress are to fire a gun, when Mr. Holmes with the other boats under his command are immediately to go to their relief, take them to the shore, or give such other assistance as he thinks may be best. When the wind blows hard, so that the boats cannot keep their order, a red flag will be hoisted in the Major's boat; then the boats are not to mind their order, but put after the flag as fast as possible to the place of landing, to which the flag-boat will always be a guide.

It is recommended to the soldiers as well as officers, not to mind the waves of the lake; but when the surf is high to stick to their oars, and the men at helm to keep the boat quartering on the waves, and briskly follow, then no mischief will happen by any storm whatever. Ten of the best steersmen amongst the Rangers are to attend Captain Campbell and company in his boats. It is Likewise recommended to the officers commanding in those boats, to hearken to the steersmen in a storm or bad weather, in managing their boats. At evening (if it is thought neccessary to row in the night time) a blue flag will be hoisted in the Major's boat, which is the signal for the boats to dress, and then proceed in the following manner: the boats next the hindermost, are to wait for the two in the rear, the two third boats for the second two; and so on to the boats leading a-head, to prevent separation, which in the night would be hazardous.

Mr Brheme is not to mind the order of march, but to steer as is most convenient for him to make his observations; he is however desired never to go more than a league a-head of the detachment, and is to join them at landing or encamping.

On landing, the Regulars are to encamp in the center, and Lieutenant Holmes's division on the right wing with Mr. Croghan's people, Lieutenant McCormick on the left wing with his division; Mr. Jequipe to be always ready with his Mohegan Indians, which are the picquet of the detachment, part of which are always to encamp in the front of the party; Capt. Campbell will mount a guard consisting of one Subaltern, one Serjeant, and thirty privates, immediately on landing, for the security of his own encampment and battoes; Lieutenant Holmes's division to keep a guard of one serjeant and ten Rangers on the right, and Lieutenant McCormick the like number on the left, and likewise to act as adjutant to the detachment, and the orderly drum to attend him, to be at the Serjeant's call. The general to beat when ordered by the Major, at which time the whole party is to prepare for embarking, the troops half an hour after, when all the guards are to be called in, and the party embark immediately after.

There is to be no firing of guns in this detachment without permission from the commanding officer, except when in distress on the lake. No man to go without the centries, when in camp, unless he has orders so to do; great care to be taken of the arms, and the officers to review them daily. Captain Campbell will order a drum to beat, for the regulation of his company when landed, at any time he thinks proper for parading his men, or reviewing their arms, &c.

It is not doubted but due attention will be paid to all orders given.

Mr. Croghan will, at landing, always attend the Major for orders, and to give such intelligence as he may have had from the Indians throughout the day.

We left Presque Isle the 4th of November, kept a western course, and by night had advanced twenty miles.

The badness of the weather obliged us to lie by all the next day; and as the wind continued very high, we did not advance more than ten or twelve miles the 6th, on a course west-south-west.

We set out very early on the 7th, and came to the mouth of Chogage River; here we met with a party of Attawawa Indians, just arrived from Detroit. We informed them of our success in the total reduction of Canada, and that we were going to bring off the French garrison at Detroit, who were included in the capitulation. I held out a belt, and told them I would take my brothers by the hand, and carry them to Detroit, to see the truth of what I had said. They retired, and held a council, and promised an answer next morning. That evening we smoaked the calamet, or pipe of peace, all the officers and Indians smoaking by turns out of the same pipe. The peace thus concluded, we went to rest, but kept good guards, a little distrusting their sincerity.

The Indians gave their answer early in the morning, and said their young warriors should go with me, while the old ones staid to hunt for their wives and children.

I gave them ammunition at their request, and a string of

wampum in testimony of my approbation, and charged them to send some of their sachems, or chiefs, with the party who drove the oxen along shore; and they promised to spread the news, and prevent any annoyance from their hunters.

We were detained here by unfavourable weather till the 12th, during which time the Indians held a plentiful market in our camp of venison and turkies.

From this place we steered one mile west, then a mile south, then four miles west, then south-west ten miles, then five miles west-and-by-south, then south-west eight miles, then west-and-by-south seven miles, then four miles west, and then south-west six miles, which brought us to Elk River, as the Indians call it, where we halted two days on account of bad weather and contrary winds.

On the 15th we embarked, and kept the following courses; west-south-west two miles, west-north-west three miles, west-by-north one mile, west two miles; here we passed the mouth of a river, and then steered west one mile, west-by-south two miles, west-by-north four miles, north-west three miles, west-north-west two miles, west-by-north ten miles, where we encamped at the mouth of a river twenty-five yards wide.

The weather did not permit us to depart till the 18th, when our course was west-by-south six miles, west-by-north four miles, west two miles; here we found a river about fifteen yards over, then proceeded west half a mile, west-south-west six miles and a half, west two miles and an half, north-west two miles, where we encamped, and discovered a river sixteen yards broad at the entrance.

We left this place the next day, steering north-west four miles, north-north-west six miles, which brought us to Sandusky Lake; we continued the same course two miles, then north-north-east half a mile, north-west a quarter of a mile, north the same distance, north-west half a mile, north-by-east one furlong, north-west-by-north one quarter of a mile, north-west-by-west one mile, west-north-west one mile, then west half a mile, where we encamped near a small river, on the east-side.

From this place I detached Mr. Brheme with a letter to Monsieur Beleter, the French commandant at Detroit, in these words:

To Capt. Beletere, or the officer commanding at Detroit.

SIR,

That you may not be alarmed at the approach of the English troops under my command, when they come to Detroit, I send forward this by Lieut. Brheme, to acquaint you, that I have Gen. Amherst's orders to take possession of Detroit, and such other posts as are in that district, which, by capitulation, agreed to and signed by the Marquis de Vaudreuil, and his Excellency Major Gen. Amherst, the 8th of September last, now belong to the King of Great Britain.

I have with me the Marquis de Vaudreuil's letters to you directed, for your guidance on this occasion, which letters I shall deliver you when I arrive at or near your post, and shall encamp the troops I have with me at some distance from the fort, till you have reasonable time to be made acquainted with the Marquis de Vaudreuil's instructions, and the capitulation, a copy of which I have with me likewise. I am,

SIR,

Your humble servant,

Robert Rogers.

The land on the south-side of Lake Erie, from Presque Isle, puts on a very fine appearance; the country level, the timber tall, and of the best sort, such as oak, hickerie and locust; and for game, both for plenty and variety, perhaps exceeded by no part of the world.

162

I followed Mr. Brheme on the 20th, and took a course north-west four miles and an half, south-west two, and west three, to the mouth of a river in breadth 300 feet.

Here we found several Huron sachems, who told me, "that a body of 400 Indian warriors was collected at the entrance into the great streight, in order to obstruct our passage; and that Monsieur Beletert had excited them to defend their country: that they were messengers to know my business, and whether the person I had sent forward had reported the truth, that Canada was reduced." I confirmed this account, and that the fort at Detroit was given up by the French Governor. I presented them a large belt, and spoke to this effect:

Brothers,

With this belt I take you by the hand. You are to go directly to your brothers assembled at the mouth of the river, and tell them to go to their towns till I arrive at the fort. I shall call you there as soon as Monsieur Beleter is sent away, which shall be in two days after my arrival. We will then settle all matters. You live happily in your own country. Your brothers have long desired to bring this about. Tell your warriors to mind their fathers (the French) no more, for they are all prisoners to your brothers (the English), who pitied them, and left them their houses and goods, on their swearing by the Great One who made the world, to become as Englishmen forever. They are now your brothers; if you abuse them, you affront me, unless they behave ill. Tell this to your brothers the Indians. What I say is truth. When we meet at Detroit I will convince you it is all true.

These sachems set out in good temper the next morning, being the 21st; but as the wind was very high, we did not move from this place.

On the 22nd we encamped on a beach, after having steered

that day north-west six miles, north-north-west four, to a river of the breadth of twenty yards, then north-west-by west two miles, west-north-west-one, west four, and west-north-west five; it was with great difficulty we could procure any fuel here, the west-side of the Lake Erie abounding with swamps.

We rowed ten miles the next day, on a course north-west and by west, to Point Cedar, and then formed a camp; here we met some of the Indian messengers, to whom we had spoken two days before: they told us, their warriors were gone up to Monsieur Beleter, who, they said, is a strong man, and intends to fight you; a sachem of the Attawawas was amongst them. All their Indians set out with us. The 24th we went north-west and by north ten miles, and fourteen miles north-east, to a long point; this night sixty of the Indian party came to our camp, who congratulated us on our arrival in their country, and offered themselves as an escort to Detroit, from whence they came the day before. They informed me, that Mr. Brheme and his party were confined; and Monsieur Beleter had set up an high flag-staff, with a wooden effigy of a man's head on the top, and upon that a crow; that the crow was to represent himself, the man's head mine, and the meaning of the whole, that he would scratch out my brains. This artifice, however, had no effect; for the Indians told him (as they said) that the reverse would be the true explanation of the sign.

After we had proceeded six miles north-east, we halted at the request of the Indians, who desired me to call in the chief Captains of the party at the Streight's mouth. I did so, and spent the 26th at the same place, in conciliating their savage minds to peace and friendship.

The morning of the 27th, Monsieur Beleter sent me the following letter by Monsieur Babee.

Monsieur,

J'ai reçu la lettre que vous m'avez écrite par un de vos Officiers; comme je n'ai point d'interprete, je ne puis faire la reponse amplement.

L'Officier qui m'a remise la votre, me fait savoir qu'il étoit detaché afin de m'anoncer votre arrivé, pour prendre possession de cette garison, selon la capitulation fait en Canada, que vous avez conjointement avec un lettre de Monsiuer de Vaudreuil à mon addresse. Je vous prie, Monsieur, d'arrêter vos troupes à l'entrance de la riviere, jusques à ce que vous m'envoyés la capitulation & la lettre de Monseigneur le Marquis de Vaudreuil, afin de pouvoir y conformer.

Je suis bien surpris qu'on ne m'a pas envoyé un Officier François avec vous, selon la coûtome.

J'ai l'honneur d'étre, &c. &c.

De Beleter.

A Monsieur Monsieur *Rogers,*
Major, & commandant le
detachment Anglois.

In English thus.

Sir,

I received the letter you wrote me by one of your officers; but, as I have no interpreter, cannot fully answer it.

The officer that delivered me yours, gives me to understand, that he was sent to give me notice of your arrival to take possession of this garrison, according to the capitulation made in Canada; that you have likewise a letter from Mons. Vaudreuil directed to me. I beg, Sir, you'll halt your troops at the entrance to the river, till you send me the capitulation and the Marquis de Vaudreuil's letter, that I may act in conformity thereto.

I am surprised there is no French Officer sent to me along with you, as is the custom on such occasions.

I have the honour to be, &c. &c.

De Beleter.

To *Mr. Rogers,*
Major and Commander of the
English detachment.

Shortly after a French party, under Captain Burrager, beat a parley on the west-shore; I sent Mr McCormick to know his business, who returned with the officer and the following letter:

Detroit, le 25me Novembre, 1760.

MONSIEUR,

Je vous ai déja marqué par Monsieur Burrager les raisons pourquoi je ne puis répondre en détail à la lettre qui m'a été remise le 22me du courant, par l'Officier que vous m'avez detaché.

J'ignore les raisons pourquoi il n'a voulu retourner auprès de vous. J'ai envoyé mon interprete Huron chez cette nation, que l'on me dit être attroupé sur le chemin de les contenir, ne saçhant positivement si c'est à vous ou à nous qu'ils en veuillent, & pour leur dire de ma part, qu'ils ayent a se tenir tranquilement; que je savois ce que je devois à mon General, & que de lorsque l'acte de la capitulation seroit reglé, j'étois obligé d'obéir. Le dit interprete a ordre de vous attendre, & de vous remettre la present. Ne soyez point surpris, Monsieur, si sur le long de la côte vous trouvez nos habitans sur leur garde, on leur a annoncé qu'il y avoit beaucoup de nations à votre suite, à qui on avois promis le pillage, & que lesdites nations étoient même determinées à vous le demander; je leur ai permis de regarder, c'est pour vôtre conservation & sureté ainsi que pour la nôtre, en cas que les dites nations devenoient à faire les insolents, vous seul ne seriez peut-être pas dans les circonstances presentes en état de les reduire. Je me flatte, Monsieur, que si tôt que la present vour sera parvenue, vous voudriez bien m'envoyer par quelqu'un de vos Messieurs, &

la capitulation & la lettre de Monsieur Vaudreuil. J'ai
l'honneur d'être,

MONSIEUR,

Votre tres-humble & obeissant serviteur,

Pign. de Beletere.

A Monsieur Monsieur *Rogers,*
Major, commandant le detachment
Anglois au bas de la riviere.

In English thus:

Detroit, 25th Nov. 1760.

SIR,

I have already by Mr. Barrager acquainted you with
the reasons why I could not answer particularly the letter
which was delivered me the 22d instant by the Officer
you sent to me.

I am entirely unacquainted with the reasons of his
not returning to you. I sent my Huron interpreter to
that nation, and told him to stop them, should they be
on the road, not knowing positively whether they were
inclined to favour you or us, and to tell them from me
they should behave peaceably; that I knew what I owed
to my General, and that when the capitulation should
be settled I was obliged to obey. The said interpreter has
orders to wait on you, and deliver you this.

Be not surprised, Sir, if along the coast you find
the inhabitants upon their guard; it was told them you
had several Indian nations with you, to whom you had
promised permission to plunder, nay, that they were even
resolved to force you to it. I have therefore allowed the
said inhabitants to take to their arms, as it is for your
safety and preservation as well as ours; for should these
Indians become insolent, you may not perhaps, in your
present situation, be able to subdue them alone.

I flatter myself, Sir, that, as soon as that shall come to hand, you will send me by some of the Gentlemen you have with you, both the capitulation and Monsieur Vaudreuil's letter. I have the honour to be,

SIR,

Your very humble and obedient servant,

To Major Rogers.   *Pign. Beletere.*

We encamped the next day five miles up the river, having rowed against the wind; and on the 29th I dispatched Captain Campbell, with Messieurs Barrager and Babee, and their parties, with this letter.

SIR,

I acknowledge the receipt of your two letters, both of which were delivered to me yesterday. Mr. Brheme has not yet returned. The inclosed letter from the Marquis de Vaudreuil will inform you of the surrender of all Canada to the King of Great Britain, and of the great indulgence granted to the inhabitants; as also of the terms granted to the troops of his Most Christian Majesty. Captain Campbell, whom I have sent forward with this letter, will shew you the capitulation. I desire you will not detain him, as I am determined, agreeable to my instructions from General Amherst, speedily to relieve your post. I shall stop the troops I have with me at the hither end of the town till four o'clock, by which time I expect your answer; your inhabitants under arms will not surprise me, as yet I have seen no other in that position, but savages waiting for my orders. I can assure you, Sir, the inhabitants of Detroit shall not be molested, they and you complying with the capitulation, but be protected in the quiet and peaceable possession of their estates; neither shall they be pillaged by my Indians, nor by your's that have joined me.

To Capt. Beletere,   R. Rogers.
commanding at Detroit.

I landed half a mile short of the fort, and fronting it, where I drew up my detachment on a field of grass. Here Capt. Campbell joined me, and with him came a French officer, to inform me that he bore Monsieur Beletere's compliments, signifying he was under my command. From hence I sent Lieutenants Leslie and McCormack, with thirty-six Royal Americans, to take possession of the fort. The French garrison laid down their arms, English colours were hoisted, and the French taken down, at which about 700 Indians gave a shout, merrily exulting in their prediction being verified, that the crow represented the English.

They seemed amazed at the submissive salutations of the inhabitants, expressed their satisfaction at our generosity in not putting them to death, and said they would always for the future fight for a nation thus favoured by Him that made the world.

I went into the fort, received a plan of it, with a list of the stores, from the commanding officer, and by noon of the 1st of December we had collected the militia, disarmed them, and to them also administered the oaths of allegiance.

The interval from this time to the 9th was spent in preparing to execute some measures that appeared to be necessary to the service we were upon. I put Monsieur Beletere and the other prisoners under the care of Lieut. Holmes and thirty Rangers, to be carried to Philadelphia; and ordered Capt. Campbell and his company to keep possession of the fort. Lieut. Butler and Ensign Wait were sent with a detached party of twenty men, to bring the French troops from the forts Miamie and Gatanois. I ordered, that, if possible, a party should subsist at the former this winter, and give the earliest notice at Detroit of the enemy's motions in the country of the Illinois. I sent Mr. McGee with a French officer, for the French troops at the Shawanese town on the Ohio. And as provisions were scarce, directed Capt Brewer to repair with the greatest part of the Rangers to Niagara, detaining Lieut. McCormack with thirty-seven more, to go with me to Michlimakana.

I made a treaty with several tribes of Indians living in the neighbouring country; and having directed Capt. Wait, just arrived from Niagara, to return again thither immediately, I set out for Lake Huron, and on the night of the 10th encamped at the north-end of the little Lake St. Clair, and the next evening on the west-side of the streight, at the entrance of a considerable river, where many Indians were hunting. We opened Lake Huron the day following, and saw many Indian hunters on both sides of the mouth of the streights. We coasted along the west-shore of the Lake, about twenty miles north-by-north-west, the next day being the 13th forty, and the 15th thirty-eight miles, passing the cakes of ice with much difficulty. We could not advance all the 16th, a heavy north-wind setting the cakes of ice on the south-shore in such quantities, that we could find no passage between them. I consulted the Indians about a journey to Michlimakana across by land; but they declared it impracticable at this season without snow-shoes, and to our great mortification we were obliged to return to Detroit; the ice obstructing us so much, that, with the greatest diligence and fatigue, we did not arrive there till the 21st.

I delivered the ammunition to Capt. Campbell, and on the 23d set out fot Pittsburg, marching along the west-end of Lake Erie, till the 2d of January 1761, when we arrived at Lake Sandusky.

I have a very good opinion of the soil from Detroit to this place; it is timbered principally with white and black oaks, hickerie, locusts, and maple. We found wild apples along the west-end of Lake Erie, some rich savannahs of several miles extent, without a tree, but cloathed with jointed grass near six feet high, which, rotting there every year, adds to the fertility of the soil. The length of Sandusky is about fifteen miles from east to west, and about six miles across it. We came to a town of the Windot Indians, where we halted to refresh.

On January 3d, south-east-by-east three miles, east-by-south one mile and a half, south-east a mile through a meadow, crossed a small creek about six yards wide, running east, travelled south-east-by-east one mile, passed thro' Indian houses, south-east three quarters of a mile, and came to a small Indian town of about ten houses. There is a remarkable fine spring at this place, rising out of the side of a small hill with such force, that it boils above the ground in a column three feet high. I imagine it discharges ten hogsheads of water in a minute. From this town our course was south-south-east three miles, south two miles, crossed a brook about five yards wide, running east-south-east, travelled south one mile, crossed a brook about four yards wide, running east-south-east, travelled south-south-east two miles, crossed a brook about eight yards wide. This day we killed plenty of deer and turkies on our march and encamped.

On the 4th we travelled south-south-east one mile, and came to a river about twenty-five yards wide, crossed the river, where are two Indian houses, from thence south-by-east one mile, south-south-east one mile and a half, south-east two miles, south-south-east one mile, and came to an Indian house, where there was a family of Windots hunting, from thence south-by-east a quarter of a mile, south five miles, came to the river we crossed this morning; the course of the river here is west-north-west. This day killed several deer and other game, and encamped.

On the 5th travelled south-south-west half a mile, south one mile, south-south-west three quarters of a mile, south half a mile, crossed two small brooks running east, went a south-south-west course half a mile, south half a mile, south-east half a mile, south two miles, south-east one mile, south half a mile, crossed a brook running east-by-north, travelled south-by-east half a mile, south-south-east two miles, south-east three quarters of a mile, south-south-east one mile, and came to Maskongom Creek, about eight yards wide, crossed the creek, and encamped about thirty yards from it. This day killed deer and turkies in our march.

On the 6th we travelled about fourteen or fifteen miles, our general course being about east-south-east, killed plenty of game, and encamped by a very fine spring.

The 7th our general course about south-east, travelled about six miles, and crossed Maskongom Creek, running south, about twenty yards wide. There is an Indian town about twenty yards from the creek, on the east-side, which is called the Mingo Cabbins. There were but two or three Indians in the place, the rest were hunting. These Indians have plenty of cows, horses, hogs, &c.

The 8th, halted at this town to mend our mogasons, and kill deer, the provisions I brought from Detroit being entirely expended. I went a-hunting with ten of the Rangers, and by ten o'clock had more venison than we had occasion for.

On the 9th travelled about twelve miles, our general course being about south-east, and encamped by the side of a long meadow, where there were a number of Indians hunting.

The 10th, about the same course, we travelled eleven miles, and encamped, having killed in our march this day three bears and two elks.

The 11th, continuing near the same course, we travelled thirteen miles and encamped, where were a number of Wiandots and Six Nation Indians hunting.

The 12th, travelled six miles, bearing rather more to the east, and encamped. This evening we killed several beaver.

The 13th, travelled about north-east six miles, and came to the Delaware's town, called Beaver town. This Indian town stands on good land, on the west-side of the Maskongom River; and opposite to the town, on the east-side, is a fine river, which discharges itself into it. The latter is about thirty yards wide, and the Maskongom about forty; so that when they both join, they make a very fine stream, with a swift current, running to the south-west. There are about 3000 acres of cleared ground round this place The number of warriors in this town is about 180. All the way from the Lake Sandusky I found level land, and a good country. No pine-trees of any sort; the timber is white, black, and yellow oak, black and white walnut, cyprus, chesnut, and locust trees. At this town I staid till the 16th in the morning to refresh my party, and procured some corn from the Indians to boil with our venison.

On the 16th we marched nearly an east course about nine miles, and encamped by the side of a small river.

On the 17th kept much the same course, crossing several rivulets and creeks. We travelled about twenty miles, and encamped by the side of a small river.

On the 18th we travelled about sixteen miles an easterly course, and encamped by a brook.

The 19th, about the same general course, we crossed two considerable streams of water, and some large hills timbered with chesnut and oak, and having travelled about twenty miles, we encamped by the side of a small river, at which place were a number of Delawares hunting.

On the 20th, keeping still an easterly course, and having much the same travelling as the day before, we advanced on our journey about nineteen miles, which brought us to Beaver Creek, where are two or three Indian houses, on the west side of the creek, and in sight of the Ohio.

Bad weather prevented our journeying on the 21st, but the next day we prosecuted our march. Having crossed the creek, we travelled twenty miles, nearly south-east, and encamped with a party of Indian hunters.

On the 23rd we came again to the Ohio, opposite to Fort Pitt, from whence I ordered Lieut. McCormack to march the party across the country to Albany, and, after tarrying there till the 26th, I came the common road to Philadelphia, from thence to New York, where, after this long, fatiguing tour, I arrived February 14, 1761.

Finis

ADVERTISEMENT

It is proposed to continue this Journal, in a second volume, containing an account of my travels into the country of the Cherokees, and the southern Indians; of my second tour into the interior country, upon the great lakes; and of the Indian wars in America since the year 1760; together with correct plans of all the British forts upon the continent. To be published by subscription.

Subscriptions are taken in by John Millan, Bookseller, near Whitehall, and by such others as he shall appoint, he being impowered by me for that purpose, and will give proper receipts to deliver the said volume, or return the subscription-money, within a limited time.

The price to subscribers will be one English Guinea; one half to be paid at subscribing, and the other on delivery of the book.

ALSO FROM LEONAUR

AVAILABLE IN SOFTCOVER OR HARDCOVER WITH DUST JACKET

EW2 EYEWITNESS TO WAR SERIES
CAPTAIN OF THE 95th (Rifles) *by Jonathan Leach*

An officer of Wellington's Sharpshooters during the
Peninsular, South of France and Waterloo Campaigns
of the Napoleonic Wars.

SOFTCOVER : **ISBN 1-84677-001-7**
HARDCOVER : **ISBN 1-84677-016-5**

WFI THE WARFARE FICTION SERIES
NAPOLEONIC WAR STORIES
by Sir Arthur Quiller-Couch

Tales of soldiers, spies, battles & Sieges from the
Peninsular & Waterloo campaigns

SOFTCOVER : **ISBN 1-84677-003-3**
HARDCOVER : **ISBN 1-84677-014-9**

EWI EYEWITNESS TO WAR SERIES
RIFLEMAN COSTELLO *by Edward Costello*

The adventures of a soldier of the 95th (Rifles) in the Peninsular
& Waterloo Campaigns of the Napoleonic wars.

SOFTCOVER : **ISBN 1-84677-000-9**
HARDCOVER : **ISBN 1-84677-018-1**

MCI THE MILITARY COMMANDERS SERIES
JOURNALS OF ROBERT ROGERS OF THE
RANGERS *by Robert Rogers*

The exploits of Rogers & the Rangers in his own words
during 1755-1761 in the French & Indian War.

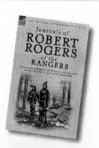

SOFTCOVER : **ISBN 1-84677-002-5**
HARDCOVER : **ISBN 1-84677-010-6**

AVAILABLE ONLINE AT
www.leonaur.com
AND OTHER GOOD BOOK STORES

LEONAUR

ALSO FROM LEONAUR
AVAILABLE IN SOFTCOVER OR HARDCOVER WITH DUST JACKET

RGW1 RECOLLECTIONS OF THE GREAT WAR 1914 - 18
STEEL CHARIOTS IN THE DESERT *by S. C. Rolls*

The first world war experiences of a Rolls Royce armoured car driver with the Duke of Westminster in Libya and in Arabia with T.E. Lawrence.

SOFTCOVER : **ISBN 1-84677-005-X**
HARDCOVER : **ISBN 1-84677-019-X**

RGW2 RECOLLECTIONS OF THE GREAT WAR 1914 - 18
WITH THE IMPERIAL CAMEL CORPS IN THE GREAT WAR *by Geoffrey Inchbald*

The story of a serving officer with the British 2nd battalion against the Senussi and during the Palestine campaign.

SOFTCOVER : **ISBN 1-84677-007-6**
HARDCOVER : **ISBN 1-84677-012-2**

EW3 EYEWITNESS TO WAR SERIES
THE KHAKEE RESSALAH
by Robert Henry Wallace Dunlop

Service & adventure with the Meerut Volunteer Horse During the Indian Mutiny 1857-1858.

SOFTCOVER : **ISBN 1-84677-009-2**
HARDCOVER : **ISBN 1-84677-017-3**

WF1 THE WARFARE FICTION SERIES
NAPOLEONIC WAR STORIES
by Sir Arthur Quiller-Couch

Tales of soldiers, spies, battles & Sieges from the Peninsular & Waterloo campaigns

SOFTCOVER : **ISBN 1-84677-003-3**
HARDCOVER : **ISBN 1-84677-014-9**

AVAILABLE ONLINE AT
www.leonaur.com
AND OTHER GOOD BOOK STORES

LEONAUR

ALSO FROM LEONAUR
AVAILABLE IN SOFTCOVER OR HARDCOVER WITH DUST JACKET

SF1 CLASSIC SCIENCE FICTION SERIES
BEFORE ADAM & Other Stories
by Jack London

Volume 1 of The Collected Science Fiction & Fantasy of Jack London.

SOFTCOVER   : **ISBN 1-84677-008-4**
HARDCOVER   : **ISBN 1-84677-015-7**

SF2 CLASSIC SCIENCE FICTION SERIES
THE IRON HEEL & Other Stories
by Jack London

Volume 2 of The Collected Science Fiction & Fantasy of Jack London.

SOFTCOVER   : **ISBN 1-84677-004-1**
HARDCOVER   : **ISBN 1-84677-011-4**

SF3 CLASSIC SCIENCE FICTION SERIES
THE STAR ROVER & Other Stories
by Jack London

Volume 3 of The Collected Science Fiction & Fantasy of Jack London.

SOFTCOVER   : **ISBN 1-84677-006-8**
HARDCOVER   : **ISBN 1-84677-013-0**

WF1 THE WARFARE FICTION SERIES
NAPOLEONIC WAR STORIES
by Sir Arthur Quiller-Couch

Tales of soldiers, spies, battles & Sieges from the Peninsular & Waterloo campaigns

SOFTCOVER   : **ISBN 1-84677-003-3**
HARDCOVER   : **ISBN 1-84677-014-9**

AVAILABLE ONLINE AT
www.leonaur.com
AND OTHER GOOD BOOK STORES

Printed in the United States
154383LV00002B/23/A

9 781846 770104